WITHDRAWN

The Civility of Indifference

F. G. BAILEY

The
Civility
of
Indifference

On Domesticating Ethnicity

CORNELL UNIVERSITY PRESS

ITHACA AND LONDON

First published 1996 by Cornell University Press.

Printed in the United States of America

♾ The paper in this book meets the minimum requirements
of the American National Standard for Information Sciences—
Permanence of Paper for Printed Library Materials, ANSI Z39.48-1984.

Library of Congress Cataloging-in-Publication Data

Bailey, F. G. (Frederick George)
    The civility of indifference : on domesticating ethnicity / F. G. Bailey.
        p.   cm.
    Includes bibliographical references and index.
    ISBN 0-8014-3217-0 (alk. paper). —ISBN 0-8014-8308-5 (pbk. : alk. paper)
        1. Ethnicity—India—Bisipara.   2. Racism—India—Bisipara.   3. Apathy—
India—Bisipara.   4. Bisipara (India)—History.   5. Bisipara (India)—
Ethnic relations.   6. Bisipara (India)—Social conditions.   I. Title.
GN635.I4B345   1996   95-37324
305.8'0954'13—dc20

Contents

Acknowledgments

The whole text has been read by Sara Dickey and Mary K. Gilliland. I thank them for their comments and encouragement. The final chapter has gone through many recensions, which have been variously read by Roy D'Andrade, Jim Holston, Dan Linger, and Tanya Luhrmann. I thank them too and absolve them from all blame. I am grateful also to Cornell's anonymous reader, who is indeed a rare one.

F. G. B.

Preface

The setting for this story of contained ethno-racist-religious strife (the kind of bigotry that in India, when uncontained, they stigmatized as "communalism") is the village of Bisipara, which lies in the Kondmals subdivision of Phulbani district in the state of Orissa in eastern India. I was there for two years between 1952 and 1955, and again for some months in 1959. It had a population at that time of about seven hundred people. The point of the story is less the strife itself than the manner of its containment.

I began to write this memoir of Bisipara's dip toward incivility forty years after I had first gone there. What awakened the memory of hitherto unexamined events was the discovery that I could make no intuitive sense of Yugoslav "ethnic cleansing." Impulse-driven cruelty I can understand, but not cruelty that is calculated and systematic. I could not imagine what those people had in their minds.

What I knew of their misery, beyond what the media provided, came from an anthropologist who had lived in the small Croatian town of Slavonski Brod, "Slavonian Ferry" (Gilliland 1986; Olsen 1993). The town lies on the river Sava, which separates Croatia from Bosnia. The matching town across the river is Bosanski Brod, "Bosnian Ferry." The old Serbian border is about fifty miles to the east. In 1983 the people of Slavonski Brod presented themselves as an amiable ethnic mix of Croats, Muslims,

ix

Serbs, and a few Slovenes, intermarried, intermingled in the workplace, sharing neighborhoods and neighborliness, certainly aware of ethnic differences but on the surface no more ethnically prejudiced than was signaled by jokes, stereotypes, and some apprehension about being sent to do military service in Kosovo, then an autonomous region in Serbia, populated mainly by ethnic Albanians. (Gypsies alone qualified for ubiquitous everyday malevolent discrimination.)

By the early 1990s most of that robustly tolerant ambience had gone. Men were away fighting in one or another army; marriages had broken; households had been dispersed as members fled to whatever they claimed to be an ethnic homeland, or to refugee camps in Italy or elsewhere. I do not understand, in the empathic sense of that word, how good-natured neighbors could so quickly and so thoroughly be turned into demonized adversaries. How did the mild pride in being Yugoslav, the patriotic and seemingly affectionate memory of Tito, the taken-for-granted pragmatism that helped people cope with their everyday life, the habitual tolerance of ethnic differences and the plural society, and the equally relaxed acceptance of the official (and unifying) Tito-communist ideology all vanish so swiftly and so completely, to be replaced by the utter mindlessness of true-believing perpetrators of genocide? I cannot empathize with such attitudes and actions, or with that unexamined righteousness.

So the Yugoslav catastrophe led me back to Bisipara, as I had known it forty years earlier. I thought the comparison might enlighten me; it did, but not as I expected. What was done in Bisipara did not explain Yugoslavia or Rwanda or any other place where ethnic strife gets out of hand. Writing this story has not done much to clarify ethnic cleansing and other such obscenities; there are, as the reader will see, too many variables involved to make the comparison useful. In fact, the process worked the other way; it made very clear to me what kind of people they were who lived in Bisipara. I see them better now because I was driven to ask the negative question. Why did they *not* behave like Serbs and Croats and Muslims or like the Hutu and the Tutsi?

Evidently they did not see the world as those unhappy peoples do. At the time I knew them, Bisipara people appeared to have nothing in common with genocidal maniacs: they were normal, seemingly with the usual complement of good and evil, and certainly given more to tolerance than to bigotry. They were, however, racists; they saw one another, quite literally, as different breeds, and they arranged these breeds in a hierarchy of worthiness. They strongly disapproved of miscegenation. The term *race*, as a way to describe the divisions in their society—a caste system—has been out of fashion for the past sixty years, deservedly so because it suggests a biological entity that does not exist (de facto miscegenation is everywhere, even in a caste society) and because it promotes a system of evaluating people that is (as I see it) both erroneous and morally offensive. *Ethnic*, implying cultural differences rather than innate capacities, is now the approved adjective. But in Bisipara they surely saw their differences as bred in the bone; they also, like racists anywhere, were unwaveringly judgmental about the differences.

But they were not obsessed by race. Their discourse on difference in breeding and culture, although firmly moralistic, was domesticated; that is, it was kept under control. Bisipara people were too worldly to let that kind of prejudice dominate their every action and do them the harm it has done in other places. Their racism was, for the most part, innocuous. I do not mean that they were, by nature, more compassionate than other people; they were not. In reality they had no choice: their perception of the world and of what they must do to survive in it was such that a mindless and uncompromising and malignant racism enacted as ethnic cleansing, had they been able to imagine it, would have been judged a disastrous indulgence, a stupidity, and a way to destroy themselves.

But I did not hear them say this; moderation and chaos, as clear alternatives, were never articulated. The rule that required them to show self-restraint was, so to speak, subliminal, part of their collective consciousness but unspoken, and apparent to me (more now than then) only in the way they conducted themselves. They observed the proprieties. Ritualized politeness shaped their public discourse, and when they interacted informally with one another they displayed careful attention to the etiquette of status. Sometimes they slipped and tempers showed, but the reaction of bystanders and perpetrators alike indicated clearly that this was bad form. Of course it is possible that I am projecting onto them attitudes and ideas that they did not in fact possess (I will come to that question later), but, for sure, the story (and the social structure it allegorizes) will make sense only if one realizes that their commonsensical pragmatism, their refusal to go to excess, their prudently concealed disrespect for officials, their dispassionate contempt for heroic posturing, and their wariness when asked to sacrifice personal interests for the common good were all habitual attitudes, unquestioned, taken for granted, not subject to open debate.

They lived out their lives in conditions that would seem unbearable to anyone raised in the better-off segments of European or American society. Bisipara people, I know, did not find life easy. But they were patient, generally phlegmatic, living mostly from day to day, not so much resigned to misery as careful to limit effort to where they believed it would be effective. They were calculators, pragmatists, quotidian thinkers, in the habit of working out consequences when they made decisions. They did not theorize; they were not philosophers. Abstract reflection on the meaning of existence or on God's design for the universe was not their thing. In fact, they had no choice but to live the "unexamined life"; unlike Socrates, they had calloused hands. Nor did they entertain themselves by imagining alternative lifestyles or contemplating economic reforms that might make life better. They did not question—at least not of their own accord—their customary ways and the shape of their society. Certainly they were entirely innocent of the impassioned moral intensity that is needed to fire social reform. I cannot imagine them willing to die (or to kill) for a principle or a cause. In short, to use an antique phrase, they lacked revolutionary potential.

Whether or not that is still the case in Bisipara I do not know. Their moderation, obviously, was not a fact of nature; it was *second* nature, located in the (at that time) undebated part of Bisipara's culture. It was not set in stone.

This memoir is written to complement *The Witch-Hunt; or, The Triumph of Morality*, which also is about Bisipara, and in particular to underline the irony of that title and the likely hypocrisy of those who presented themselves as defending morality. The present tale could have been subtitled *Morality's Defeat* and offered as an apologue—and as a paradox—to show that such a defeat is by no means always a disaster. (The morality to which I refer is that of the true believer, the fanatic who knows with absolute certainty where truth and virtue lie.)

There is an element of parable both in this and in the earlier story. What is the point of writing about others if we cannot, by doing so, better see ourselves? But the allegory is a secondary matter. So is the analysis of Bisipara's version of racial prejudice. My primary concern, in both these stories, is to memorialize Bisipara and its people, as I saw them forty years ago.

F. G. BAILEY

Del Mar, California

The Civility of Indifference

The Shiva temple in Bisipara.

1

The Temple Entry Act

In the Beginning

The earliest episode that I can find featuring Bisipara ("Bissipurra") occurred in March 1846, when Lt. Macpherson, on his fifth season of campaigning in the Kond hills, got into hot water there. Since 1835 the East India Company, which then ruled much of India, had been making small military forays into the Kond hills, at that time beyond the Company's administered domains.[1] The intention was to stamp out the Kond ritual of human sacrifice and the custom of female infanticide. Lt. Macpherson had camped at Bisipara and the Konds of the neighborhood had delivered to him 172 *meriahs* (people dedicated as victims for sacrifice to Tana Penu, the Earth divinity).[2] That same night the Konds grew restive and the next day they demanded the return of their victims, for they had been told (by various interested parties) that surrendering the victims was an act of submission that would surely be followed by taxes on their land. One of

---

[1] The East India Company (henceforth "the Company"), in origin a trading organization chartered by Queen Elizabeth in 1600, was the de facto ruler of British possessions in India until 1858, when, following the uprising of 1857–58, all its rights in India were transferred to the Crown.

[2] The word may be derived from the Oriya *mera*, which is a stake (to which victims were tied). In the Kond language, the rite is *mrimi* and the victim is *mrimi gandi*.

those stirring up the Konds was a member of the royal house of Boad, an Oriya kingdom lying to the north of the Kondmals in the Mahanadi river valley. "This absurd notion," Macpherson's memorialist (his elder brother) wrote, "was produced by the machinations of Kurtivas, the Rajah's uncle, but of illegitimate birth; who, having once held and abused the chief power in Boad, desired to involve the Khonds in difficulties with the Government, and so to increase his own importance and recover his former position."[3] The victims were handed back—later some of them were retrieved—and Macpherson beat a prudent retreat to the south in the direction of his base on the coastal plain of Orissa. This incident and its subsequent disorders led to his removal from office in March 1847 and to an inquiry, which exonerated him (in October 1848) from all charges. The command passed to another Scot, Captain Campbell, a veteran of earlier expeditions into the region.[4]

Two reports in 1848, written by Campbell, refer in passing to

[3] Macpherson 1865, 246. "I take this early opportunity," Evans-Prichard wrote in *The Nuer* (1940, 9n. 1), "to inform readers that I have not spelt Nuer names and other words with phonetic consistency. I raise no objection, therefore, to anyone spelling them differently." I, too, am permissive in this matter (and, I hope, similarly disarming). Nineteenth-century spelling of the word I write as *Kond* is usually *Khond*, sometimes *Kandh* or *Khanda*. In fact, not the *k* but the *d* is aspirated in the Oriya word, so that *Kondh* would be nearer the mark. (The Kond name for themselves and their language is *Kui*.) *Boad* phonetically would be better written as *Bauddh*, which most speakers of English would not know how to pronounce. Names easily (if imperfectly) pronounced are better remembered; the story matters, not phonetic niceties.

[4] Campbell's comments (in books published in 1861 and 1864), both on this incident and on Macpherson's articles about the Kond religion in the *Calcutta Review*, led to an acrimonious interchange between Campbell and Macpherson's brother, William. In 1865 the latter published a substantial memoir of his brother, Samuel, who had died in 1860. The elder Macpherson was particularly incensed by an anonymous booklet, published in 1849, evidently written by a hack (hired by Campbell, it seems), denigrating Macpherson's accomplishments in the Kond hills, while boosting Campbell's (see *Khond Agency* 1849; Campbell 1861, 1864; Macpherson 1865). Campbell and Macpherson were among the several soldiers and civilian officers posted to the Kond hills and charged to end not only human sacrifice and female infanticide but also clan warfare. It is a minor irony that the Scottish clans of Campbell and Macpherson were hereditary enemies.

Bisipara (*Khond Agency* 1849, 61, 137). The first, in the course of paying compliments to the achievements of a Captain Hicks in, I think, 1840 or 1841, lists places in the Kondmals where Oriya chieftains with good things to say about Hicks were to be found. One of these places was "Biseparrah." The second report, dated a month later, outlines a route for a road to be built across the Kond hills from the coastal plains of Orissa to Sonepur on the upper reaches of the Mahanadi river, roughly the cultural boundary that separates Orissa from central India. "Bispurra" is listed as being ten miles from "Coinjuro" (Koinjoro, which lies to the south and east of Bisipara, upstream along the valley of the Salki river) and nine miles from "Catringia" (Katrangia, to the north and west). Today (I write of the 1950s) tracks connect these places, but so far as I know the route was never surveyed; certainly no road was built.

The reports[5] that were written at the time, and the memoirs that subsequently were published, talked about three main categories of people living in the Kond hills. The Konds, speaking their own language, Kui (which was not written), practicing a kind of religion that was soon to be labeled animism, and perpetrating the meriah ritual, were numerically dominant. Living among them were Oriyas, speakers of Oriya (the language of Orissa), migrants up from the small Hindu kingdoms that lay on the plains around the Kond hills. The Oriyas occupied fortified villages (fortifications were wooden fences eight feet high) in the wider valleys of the upland region, where the land could be leveled to construct irrigated paddy fields. In the 1950s Oriyas were about three in every eight of the population; they were probably fewer at the beginning of the nineteenth century, before the East India Company took over administration of the hill regions, established markets, and made the place safe for other Oriya immigrants who came up into the hills as traders and employees of the administration.

[5] An informative compilation is Volume 5 of *Selections from the Records of the Government of India.*

The third set of people were—and are—Panos, variously referred to as Panwas, weavers, Doms, or sometimes Pariahs.[6] In
the 1950s they were about one in six of the population. Lt. Macpherson, a diligent reporter of Kond culture and society, wrote
that "the Panwa is proverbially indispensable to every Khond
hamlet. His duties are to provide human victims, an occupation
which is, however, restricted to certain families in which it is
hereditary; to carry messages, such as summonses to council or
to the field [of battle]; to act as a musician at ceremonies, and to
supply the village with cloth. . . . [They] partake of food which
has been prepared by the Khonds, who will not, however, eat
from their hands. . . . They use both the Khond and the Oriyah
languages." He continues: "They are treated with great kindness,
but as an inferior and protected, perhaps a servile race. They are
never neglected at a feast; and any injury done to them is
promptly resented. But they are never allowed to bear themselves as equals" (1865, 65).

Bisipara, which is an Oriya village, also had quarters for its
"servile race" of Panos. In 1952 this was a street, called *Panosai*,
situated about two hundred yards across the fields to the north
and east of the metropolitan part of the village, the street of the
Warriors. Like their fellows in Kond villages, the Bisipara Panos
were "never allowed to bear themselves as equals." Macpherson's description of their position was still, in its essence, accurate in 1952. The same responsibilities, except for the kidnapping
of meriahs, were still theirs. In Bisipara the dominant group was
not Kond but an Oriya caste that I will call "Warrior," since a
literal translation of their Oriya name (the "purified ones") does
not sufficiently suggest the mastery they claim they once held
over the village and the warlike propensities that, like the Konds,
they exhibited before the region was pacified. Panos accepted
food cooked in a Warrior household, but no Warrior would eat
food prepared by Panos or even take water from them. Given

---

[6] Caste names have an initial capital letter. Thus, a Weaver belongs to that
caste; a weaver weaves cloth, which some Weavers did (some did not), and
so did some Panos.

that Warriors could make legitimate marriages only with other Warriors and that Panos could marry only Panos, Warriors and Panos were never kinfolk.

In a perfectly straightforward sense of the word, Panos were deemed by Warriors (and by people from other "clean" castes) to be *unclean*. They were untouchable, quite literally. Physical contact with a Pano polluted Warriors and made it necessary for them to take a bath (and sometimes carry out other and more stringent forms of purification) before they could enter the kitchen of their own house, eat a meal, go to a temple, draw water from a well, touch another person of clean caste—before, in short, they could function again as normal people. Quite logically, Panos were forbidden to enter the kitchen of a clean-caste house, to draw water from the well in a clean-caste street, to enter the meeting house in Warrior street where the village council (*panchayat*) met, or to go inside any of the village temples other than the one they had built in their own street.

All those disabling prohibitions make it sound as if Panos lived a life of ghettoed isolation, but in fact they were closely, even precisely, integrated into the life of the village. This was not the integration of equal opportunity that the word suggests at the present day, but an integration that is constructed out of difference, out of specialization, out of limits set by convention on the work that a person can do and the power that he or she can exercise. It is the integration that God devised when he placed the rich man in his castle and the poor man at the gate and planned for each of them to stay there, so that there might be order in the world.

Each Warrior household had attached to it one or more households of Panos. The attachment was in part economic, for the Pano's principal duty was to work in his master's fields and to perform whatever other tasks the master required. But the link was imagined in a form that was fuller, more complete, more exalted with a sense of duty and obligation than is connoted by the term *employment*. The Warrior was *raja*, the king, and the Pano was *praja*, the subject or vassal, and their relationship was marked, in theory at least, by loyalty and trust. The Pano was the Warrior's henchman, a trusted servant waiting on his master's bidding, ready to fight his master's battles, and, reciprocally, sure of his master's support and protection. A wedding or a death or severe sickness or any of the several crises that fall on households were occasions for the praja to show his loyalty by the services he provided. When similar events took place in the servant's household, the master made appropriate contributions to the cost of rituals that were performed. The relationship had in it a quasi-familial strand, a morality that was supposed to preclude calculations of advantage or considerations of profit and loss. Payment was a fixed share of the crops grown on the master's land (or sometimes a field lent to the servant to cultivate on his own account, using the master's oxen), so that the two of them shared the prosperity of good years and suffered together when harvests were bad. Furthermore, the connection between the households was supposed to hold through the generations.

Besides these links between individual Warrior families and individual Pano families, one to one, the Panos were integrated into the village as a corporate group, owning the right to exercise a particular skill; they were Bisipara's music makers. Weddings in households, and some of the many public festivals that marked Bisipara's religious year, required the services of musicians, usually four or five men beating on drums of various kinds and one or two playing the strident oboe that they call a *mohuri*. If the occasion included a feast, the musicians would receive their portion of the food that was cooked; it was also the custom in 1952 to give them a small gratuity. (The other service they provided was scavenging. No Hindu of clean caste would touch a dead cow or a dead ox. Panos took away the carcass, flayed it—they sold the leather or used it for drums and other purposes—and ate the meat. This, Bisipara people of clean caste said, was what made Panos untouchable.)

The body of the village, its essence, was the group of Warrior households. In 1952 they formed just under a fifth of Bisipara's population. (Panos, almost twenty-two percent of the village's seven hundred people, were slightly more numerous.) Warriors saw themselves as Bisipara's sceptred race, its one-time owners; all others were there as dependents. The dependents were Brahmins, Herdsmen, Potters, Distillers, Barbers, Washermen, and some others. All together, twenty-one different castes were represented in Bisipara in 1952. Many of them (but not all) had a specific task to contribute to the village, for which they were rewarded, as were the prajas, by receiving a share of the harvest.

Those, broadly speaking, were the estates that God ordered for the people of Bisipara and other Oriya villages in the Kond hills at the time when Lt. Macpherson was trying to bring to the Konds the nineteenth-century British version of good government and natural justice. This Bisipara, as yet uncomplicated by alien definitions of good government, was an agrarian society. Land, then the only significant source of wealth, belonged to one dominant group, the Warriors. Other castes got their share by serving either individual Warrior households or the village as a corporation. Wealth was concentrated; power was concentrated. But God's ordering did not, in this scheme of things, privilege the Warriors to live as despots off the suffering and deprivation of their "subaltern classes." On the contrary, there was nowhere for the wealth that flowed upwards into Warrior hands to go except down again, redistributed to the Warriors' dependents. If power was concentrated in the Warrior caste, moreover, it also was balanced by duty, by the obligation to protect the social order—the·universal order that Hindus call *dharma*. That task rested upon the Warriors, as their burden. Seen thus, they were less the owners of the community than its trustees. They did not so much enjoy privilege; rather they bore responsibility. That was how, still in the 1950s, they tried to see themselves.

A community organized that way, with power and privilege and responsibility allocated according to "race," is the very inverse of what now is thought desirable. There was, at least on Bisipara's front stage, no respect whatsoever paid to ideas that inform modern democracy or modern notions of the proper management of ethnicity. Equal opportunity to compete for

power, the monochrome identity of equal citizenship, and education into a common set of values and a common way of life were
all absent. There were some values held in common on the front
stage (for example the caste hierarchy itself), and there were
others, more covert because not articulated but most certainly
significant, which I have mentioned and will enlarge upon later.
Nevertheless, one misses the central feature of the traditional
community if one does not foreground the idea that humanity
consists of groups that are ineradicably diverse in their natures
and are ordered into a hierarchy of respect. This discontinuity,
especially between Warrior, Pano, and Kond, emerges in every
line of the texts presented below.

The nineteenth-century British imperialists who found themselves in the Kond hills (many of them, including those who
have left the fullest accounts of themselves, were Scots) surely
were not affronted by the familiar Tory notion of having a station
in life. They were also probably less cynical than are their descendents about the *noblesse oblige* that attaches to privilege.[7]
They were bemused by the intricacies of caste distinctions, and
they were comfortably outraged by the rite of human sacrifice
and the practice of female infanticide. But not everything in the
Kondmals would have been unexpected. One can read traces of
fossilized agrarian values in their discourse, particularly respect
for the life of the warrior-husbandman and a marked disdain for
commerce. More on that later.

Was that community ever the actuality? Was there ever a time
when Warriors alone owned land? Did the people of Bisipara
really live within the constraints of an order in which each and
every one of them accepted an allotted station in life? I do not
know, for there are no systematic descriptions of life in Bisipara
before I went there in 1952. But I suspect that to say yes to any of
those questions would be to confuse design with reality. Such

---

[7] William Macpherson memorialized his brother with a verse from Virgil:
"Is genus indocile ac dispersum montibus altis / Composuit, legesque dedit"
[That rude race, dispersed in the high mountains, / He pacified, and gave
them laws].

unreserved and total acceptance of any social order must be unlikely. The dominant-and-dependent-caste portrayal of life in Bisipara, which I gave above, could never have been the entire
reality. It is not a description of the way things *were* in the old
days, when people knew their places in society; it is a claim
about the way things *should be* arranged, someone's rhetoric
about the shape that God ordained for Bisipara's society. The
pattern then becomes only a *purported* description of a past
golden age, in reality a recommended model for the future and a
framework against which to justify or condemn present conduct.
Dharma, in this paradigm, is the *natural* order of things; to go
against it is not only foolish but also is sinful. This particular
dharma, obviously, is one that privileges the Warriors. (That does
not mean, it will become clear later, that other castes necessarily
rejected it.)

Claims to privilege are also made through histories, through
the narration of purported past events. In December 1953 Debohari Bisoi, a Warrior employed as a schoolmaster (a much esteemed occupation), wrote down a history of the Warrior caste,
eliciting it from a very old man, Nobino Bisoi. Here is an edited
excerpt:

The Warriors of Bisipara first came to the village of Bolscoopa
in the Kondmals. That village was a fort belonging to the Raja of
Boad. The Raja of Boad travelled across the Kondmals to attack
the fort of Mahasinghi and take the image of Durga away from
the Raja of Kimedi. After a long war he was victorious and
brought back the drum in which the deity resided. Since we
Warriors went to fight the war, we alone have the right to make
offerings to the deity at Bolscoopa.

Their numbers multiplied and after a time the Warriors came
to Bisipara. At that time twenty-two Kond families lived there,
doing many wicked things. After a long war, the Warriors, who
were great heroes and very skilled in magic, burnt the Kond
houses and drove the Konds out. The spring that now feeds the
well in Hatopodera [the old marketplace in Bisipara] was there
at that time.

The Konds who live in Domosinghi attacked over the Dolopodori mountain and they killed Bhagirathi Bisoi. Later they attacked again and Drono Bisoi fell surrounded by Konds. When his own brother Drono fell among the Konds, the great hero Ongo Bisoi crept under cover close to the Konds and let off his gun. The Konds fled and Ongo and his brother chased them and killed many of them. This was the war of Dolopodori. It must be added that Ongo and Drono, having eaten a certain substance, were invulnerable. Shot, sword, and axe could not hurt their bodies.

In this fashion time passed until the Kondmals came under British rule and the famous Dinobandu Tahsildar divided the Kondmals into fifty *muthas* [administrative units: literally, a fist, a fistful, something held] and put a *sirdar* in charge of each. Those put in charge received the title of Bisoi; previously their name was Amato.

Panos had a different version of these events in Bisipara's past. Here is the story as told by Sindhu Sahani, another schoolmaster and a Pano:

The Kondmals were at first part of Boad, and the Boad king lived at Bolscoopa. Our ancestors, Mondano and Gopalo Sahani, were leading men there. When the Raja went to Mahasinghi to seize the deity, these two men went with him, playing the mohuri and the drums.

The Konds were ignorant and uncivilized and savage. They obeyed no one. Their villages consisted of leaf houses in the jungle. Those who offended them were killed. Seeing the backwardness of the Konds, the Raja moved his residence down to Boad.

Mondano and Gopalo had very big families. It was then the custom to offer human sacrifice to the deity and the Sahani family put many heads before the deity. The population of Bolscoopa grew and they looked for a new place to live.

At that time Bisipara belonged to the Konds and was called Talopara. The Konds there had two champions, Biniki and Saniki Kohoro. No Oriyas were able to take Talopara; those that came there were killed. Four of the descendents of Mondano and Gopalo were told: "Biniki and Saniki Kohoro are killing Oriyas. Konds trust you and you can come and mingle with them and be their advisers. Make them drunk with liquor and then murder them. Then we can all settle in Bisipara together."

The Panos came and killed their foes and built houses for them-selves and made it possible for other people to settle here.

In 1841 the Kondmals came under British rule and Bisipara became the headquarters. [Events did not move quite that fast.] Panos were not educated. They did not know how to cultivate for themselves; they always got their food from others. They said, "We killed the foes of the Oriyas. Give us a potful of rice." They called the Bisoi their great lord and became his prajas.

In 1901 the British official A. J. Ollenbach came and saw that the Panos were foolish, uneducated, and poor. He built schools and taught them cultivation and gave them land. Before then, because they were hungry, Panos used to steal and have to sleep in the jail. A. J. Ollenbach, who is now dead, put a stop to this, and Panos observed the law of the sahibs. Nowadays some cul-tivate their own land, some sharecrop, some have government land, some are landless laborers, and some live by trading.

These tales were written down for me. They did not feature in everyday discourse in the village and were not subjected to di-rect arguments about relative authenticity. But they were part of village lore and the messages in them are obvious enough. They are also an indicator of how the past may be differently used to grind the axes of present-day contentiousness. I will come to those conflicts soon. Meanwhile, here is another account of the Panos. Written by Debohari Bisoi, it purports to be a summary of a longer text in the possession of Sindhu Sahani:

Among living things man is the senior. God gave man intel-ligence. First mankind was divided into four castes. These were the Brahmins, the Ksattriyas, the Baisyos and the Sudras. The Brahmins recited the Vedas, the Ksattriyas went to war, the Baisyos practiced cultivation and trade, and the Sudras were the servants of the three higher castes. These four castes could not do everything and so they were divided into many castes. Among these are the Pano caste, and their founders were Mon-dano and Gopalo Sahani. We are their descendents.

At first there were no Panos in Bisipara. Then they came here with the Warriors. Educated Hindus venerate cattle and cows, calling them "mother." Since the Panos killed cows and ate the meat and sold the skins, they are counted much lower than other castes according to the Hindu *Shastras*. If a Hindu of another caste touches one of them he goes to take a bath. They are also thieves. Their conduct is rotten. They are such that they will take filthy dead cows from Konds and eat the meat after keeping it for ten or twelve days.

The paragraph division is mine. I made it to indicate the place where I think Debohari's prejudices took editorial control of the précis writing.

A Hundred Years Forward

Lt. Macpherson and other servants of the East India Company made annual cold-season forays into the Kond hills all through the 1840s. I came to Bisipara about a century later, spending two extended periods there between 1952 and 1955 and visiting it again on several occasions in 1959. In that time I heard about (and in some instances witnessed) certain tumultuous events that seemed to signify a revolution in the community's power structure. There were threats and a good deal of posturing and the appearance of apprehension. There was some small violence, but not much.

What caught my interest, thinking later about what I had seen, was the way that people seemed more intent on getting inside their opponents' heads than on breaking them. They were putting on a show, sending a message. They were all the time looking for rhetoric (including the messages that actions convey) that would authenticate one or another definition of the social reality and make it prevail over rival definitions. Opponents were people to be manipulated into acknowledging that their version of God's design for the community was the wrong version, and sometimes the antagonists seemed to think that if they could get their own definition acknowledged as correct, actuality would conform with it. Partly they were right, for certain kinds of reality can be made and remade by definitions. Or—a variant on this—a reality can, for a time anyway, be made inoperative or at least uncertain by refusing to recognize it. The quarrel in Bisipara, at the time I witnessed it, seemed to be less about acquir-

ing control over material resources (land was still the main re-
source) than about human dignity, about getting people to acknowledge, publicly, who had control.

The peculiarly elastic connection between material power and
dignity is one issue in this story, which is in part about a contest
over legitimacy and the value the villagers set on legitimacy. (In
this context, to be legitimate means to be accorded dignity, to be
recognized as a person having specific rights. One can have
power without having legitimacy.) It will become apparent that
in Bisipara at that time legitimacy was by no means a pearl beyond price. The cultural performances that I saw—the political
theater of a struggle for power between untouchables and clean
castes—were carefully staged and insulated so that there would
be no damaging fallout on a style of life so internalized in village
habits that it needed no discursive articulation. Why those ethno-
racist loyalties did not escalate into mindless violence, as they so
often have done in India and elsewhere, is the central theme of
this essay.

In 1947 the British left India. In 1949 the government of Orissa,
along with several other Indian states and in accordance with
Gandhi's wishes, passed an act through its Legislative Assembly
making it an offence to bar Hindus from temples on the grounds
of their belonging to an untouchable caste. This was the Temple
Entry Act.

Gandhi, at a time when there was an array of generic terms to
indicate persons of untouchable status in India—outcaste, untouchable, scheduled caste, and a host of particular names such
as Dom, Pariah, Chamar, and many others—chose instead to call
all of them *Harijan*, "Child of God" (literally, "Vishnu's person").
Since, of course, everyone is a child of God, the implication is
that untouchables are in no essential way different from other
people; everyone shares the same essence.

In *A Grammar of Motives* Kenneth Burke writes, "In any term
we can posit a world, in the sense that we can treat the world *in
terms of* it, seeing all as emanations, near or far, of its light" (1969,
105). In prosaic language, he is talking ultimately about models,
paradigms, frames of reference, guiding philosophies, problem-

atics, epistemes, discursive formations—sets of assumptions available to make sense of the world of experience. More precisely, the quotation identifies labels or slogans—the entitling titles—that recommend those philosophies. Burke names these labels "God terms." (*Slogan* is from the Gaelic and means a war cry, which is an appropriate association for the argument that is to follow.) The word *Harijan* became a simplifying "God term," and through it Gandhi "posited a world."

The world he posited is in some respects quite unlike that contained in other apparently related God terms, such as *ethnicity*, *racism*, or *minority*. Those words enfold ideas, anathema to Gandhi, about power and hegemony (power exercised through convincing others that their subordination is natural and therefore right). *Harijan* also encodes some complicated ideas about *truth as relative* against *truth as absolute*, and about truth as a positive thing, empirically testable, against truth construed as a morality, what ought to be rather than what is. Gandhi did not admit those distinctions: for him truth was absolute; and there was only one truth, the truth of morality. That kind of truth is not validated empirically; once encountered, it is instantly known. In other words, it must be taken on faith; it is God's truth. *Harijan* has certain preset, nonnegotiable values, and as a result of this steadfastness the term came to be fighting talk in a campaign to combat prejudice against untouchable castes. This adversarial use of the word is an unfortunate irony, since Gandhi's wish was that all the different castes, including untouchables, should at the same time preserve their distinctiveness (marked by endogamy and specialized occupations) *and* live together in cooperation, harmony, and equality.

Since castes are inbreeding populations and acknowledged as such, caste prejudice is, by definition, a kind of racial prejudice. It is also ethnic prejudice, hostility justified on the grounds of objectionable styles of living and unacceptable modes of belief. Racial or ethnic prejudice (the separation between the two is paper-thin) has a range of expression that extends through three stages: first, mild contempt, as in jokes about the Irish, or the Jews, or the Poles, or nicknames like Jock or Taffy or Pom; second, customary or legal forms of discrimination, which may be accepted by those marked as inferior or may give rise to calculated forms of resistance that sometimes manage to change the offending laws and customs; third, the horrendous extremes of terror, lynching, and genocide. The distinctive element underlying all such stereotyping (at all three levels of intensity) is an idea that we code in terms of "blood" (nowadays also of "genetic inheritance"): the notion that worthiness or dignity or the very quality of being human is transmitted in the genes. This assumption that individuals are hard-wired to behave in a particular way then becomes the justification for privilege or debasement. Bisipara, with the Temple Entry Act, was set for the second stage of the three outlined above: law-abiding protest against customary discrimination. The Panos made a bid to have the act enforced in Bisipara.

Excluding the one that the Panos erected for themselves in their own street, there were three temples in Bisipara. One was in Market street, built by a Weaver who had once made himself rich and who was still alive in 1952, an old impoverished man, addicted to ganja, Chano Mehera. Another, in the street of the Warriors, was dedicated to Sri Ramchandro, the seventh incarnation of the god Vishnu, and was the center of village worship. It was managed by the village council. Its management—and particularly the task of replacing the dilapidated wooden building with a new construction of bricks and mortar—was a constant source of altercation in the years I was in touch with Bisipara.

The third temple lay on the southern margins of the village, a hundred yards away from Warrior street, in a grove of trees that adjoined the government inspection bungalow and a well that they called "the government well," signifying that anyone, of whatever caste, could use it. The temple was, by local standards, an imposing construction, brick-built, rendered with plaster and whitewashed, with one large and one smaller pagoda-style tower and a roofed-in forechamber. It was metropolitan in its style and dimensions, on a scale that was common enough in small townships on the plains of Orissa but rare in the Kond hills. The villagers referred to it as the Shiva temple (*Sibhomundiro*).

Inaugurating Sri Ramchandro's new "house." The picture is taken from inside the forecourt of the temple.

The Gonjagura Brahmin hired to perform the inauguration ceremony at Sri Ramchandro's temple.

A procession of Panos on their way to the Shiva temple. The garlanded portable harmonium belonged to Sindhu Sahani and was a mark of Pano modernity. No one else possessed one.

Sri Ramchandro's temple in Warrior street, as I mentioned, was a source of almost daily contention. This hub of disaccord had several spokes. The village council had quarreled with the Brahmin whose hereditary privilege it was to perform the rituals there, and in his place the council had appointed his younger brother, who was inexperienced and had to be prompted continually during the ceremonies by the displaced elder brother. Sometimes, for special occasions, they hired a Brahmin from another village, much to the elder brother's chagrin. The villagers also fell out over allocating the work to be done in constructing the new building; they took turns in stigmatizing one another as slackers and free-riders. They quarreled about the funds that were collected from time to time and accused the fundholders of stealing. But, squabbling notwithstanding, the daily rituals were performed in Sri Ramchandro's "house," along with the several major festivals that punctuated Bisipara's year. It was clearly a valued institution, a marker of the community's identity.

By contrast, Bisipara people seemed sometimes to wish that the other temple, the Sibhomundiro, were somewhere else. When the rendering peeled away from the outer wall and grass and weeds sprouted from the brickwork, they did not, as they would have done for Sri Ramchandro's temple, organize a work party to clean it up. They sent an irritated message to the man in charge, reminding him that he derived income from the temple's fields and should spend some of it maintaining the fabric. Part of the problem was divided management. A Brahmin family (of a subcaste inferior to that of the family which cared for Sri Ramchandro's temple) was charged with performing the rituals, but the appointee had died and his widow engaged other Brahmins (of a third and still less exalted subcaste) to conduct the major ceremonials. In practice most of the work, not simply the day-to-day management of the institution but also some of the rites of worship, was done by a man of the Mali caste (usually glossed as Gardener or Flower Grower), who was therefore competent, if things were rightly done, only to provide the flowers and other materials required for the services. He was the recipient of the panchayat's irate message to get the place cleaned up, appropriately so because he had a major hand in running the temple. The Mali made a good living out of people who came by to make vows and give offerings to the deity. He was, in some ways, like an altar-boy who had usurped the privilege of saying Mass and hearing confessions. I am sure the village would never have countenanced such a state of affairs for Sri Ramchandro's temple.

The temple, like its Mali manager and the Brahmin widow, was at the margins of Bisipara's community. The temple's history made it marginal. It had been built, the villagers said, by Dinobandu Tahsildar. In 1855 the Kondmals were annexed from the Raja of Boad, the nominal suzerain, and directly administered by the government. Before the first European resident official appeared on the scene (about the 1880s), the subdivision was in the charge of a "native" officer (a *tahsildar*) reporting to his superiors in Cuttack, who were three weeks' posting away (by runner).

The first tahsildar was Dinobandu Patnaik, formerly a *havildar* (sergeant) in one of the Company's native regiments. With superiors that far away, he was in practice less a bureaucrat than a lord in his own domain. Dinobandu, both the records and local traditions agree, was a brutal and avaricious man who caused much misery for the Konds and put much energy into enriching himself and his cronies. He selected Bisipara as his headquarters and—perhaps to atone for all the wicked things he did—caused the Sibhomundiro to be built there. It was built and paid for not by the people of Bisipara alone but by "all the Kondmals." No doubt the construction was done, as all public works were done in those days (and up to 1947 for certain projects), by *bheti*, which was compulsory labor paid only by provisioning the workers while they were on the job.

Some time after 1949, when the Temple Entry Act was passed, and before 1952, when I came to Bisipara, there was a disturbance at the Sibhomundiro. The occasion, I was told, was a major festival, probably the celebration of the deity's birthday, which takes place in November. It is the custom for households to bring offerings to the temple and to receive *prasad*, food dedicated to the deity and thereby made sacred. Clean-caste people entered the temple's forechamber to hand over their offerings; untouchables handed over theirs at the threshold. The households from Panosai arrived all together, as they did every year, attended by musicians, but on this occasion they demanded that the law be observed and they be allowed to enter the forechamber.

According to the tale that was told me, this confrontation was done in a manner that had become the approved political style in India. Notice of confrontation was given to those likely to oppose the move. Just as Congress politicians, intending to stage a nonviolent protest and court arrest invariably informed the authorities beforehand, so also the Panos had let it be known that on this occasion they would demand entry into the Sibhomundiro. The Warrior response was to mount a guard of men armed with battle-axes, the traditional weapon of the Kond hills, around the temple to make sure that no Pano crossed the threshold. But the Panos had taken a further step; they had informed the authorities in the district headquarters, Phulbani, about eight miles away, of what they intended to do. The result, late in the morning of the day of confrontation was the unhurried arrival in the village of the local equivalent of a riot squad consisting of a sub-inspector of police escorted by two constables, all three mounted on bicycles. If the authorities had felt a sense of urgency, it was evidently muted.

The Warrior guard stood down and the policemen were provided with refreshments (tea and *mudi*—puffed rice) by the mutha headman (the sirdar).[8] Then the leading men of the village retired with the sub-inspector to sit under a banyan tree, the Panos on one side of him and the clean castes on the other, to argue the case. I have only a bare summary of what was said. The Panos argued they were legally entitled to go inside the temple. The Warriors did not directly dispute the law, but said that they were merely the trustees of the temple, not its owners, and while they themselves would stand down and permit the Panos to go inside, they could not in good conscience do so without consulting all the other Hindus in the Kondmals, for, as everyone knew, the Sibhomundiro belonged not to Bisipara but to all the people of the Kondmals. Let the inspector sahib ("Sir Inspector") consult those other Hindus, and they, the people of Bisipara, would surely abide by the verdict.

What the sub-inspector (he happened to be a Brahmin) said to this I was not told; but I can make a guess. My guess is that he did not try to mediate, still less to risk arbitration and say who was right and who was wrong. He probably told the Panos that their proper course was to seek a remedy in the courts, if they thought their legal rights were being withheld from them. The Warriors could then, if they wished, counterpetition, arming

---

[8] This man, Bagoboto Bisoi, was sirdar of Besringia mutha. The sirdar of a neighboring mutha, Betimendi, was also a resident of Bisipara and a distant relative of the Besringia sirdar. His name was Gotikrishna Bisoi. Unless otherwise noted, "the sirdar" in the present story is always Bagoboto.

themselves with evidence that they had made the necessary consultations and could speak for all the Hindus in the Kondmals. Then, as was a policeman's habit in places like Bisipara at that time, he would have told them all, Warriors and Panos alike, that the *sircar* (administration) was very displeased and would not tolerate disorderly conduct, and if he heard any more reports of bad behavior he would station a couple of constables in the village and keep them there until the villagers learned not to cause trouble. The bite in that threat is the behavior of constables billeted out in villages; they are extremely rapacious guests.

The sub-inspector and his escort cycled back to Phulbani that afternoon, having received gifts of uncooked food (rice, lentils, and a couple of chickens). There was no more trouble of that kind that year in Bisipara. The Panos staged no more confrontations. That was the time they built the Shiva temple in their own street, under the leadership of Sindhu the schoolmaster, who himself conducted the worship there. It was a modest construction, with mud walls and a thatched roof, but they did whitewash the walls, so that the building stood out from the drab khaki houses that lined the street.

The clean castes punished their Panos by taking away the privilege of making music on festive occasions. All the time I lived in Bisipara music was provided not by the Panos of Panosai, who had come from Boad when the village was founded and were the descendents of Mondano and Gopalo Sahani, but by other Panos who came up from the Orissa plains to the south in the wake of the British. As well, a man of the Sweeper caste performed on the mohuri. Thus, in this symbolic fashion, the clean castes signified that they no longer considered Boad Panos a legitimate part of the Bisipara community.

Or perhaps they did. It is hard to be sure, because economic links, farm labor in particular, continued unchanged. Debohari, in the midst of apparently more serious troubles that erupted in 1953 and led to litigation in the government courts, contracted with three Panos to clear sand and stones washed down onto one of his paddy fields. On two occasions, in the midst of the litigation, Panos brought cases of domestic strife (one within a family and one between neighbors) to be settled by the sirdar, a Warrior, and the village council (all of them clean caste); and there may have been other such occasions that I did not record. The sirdar himself joined with a Potter and a Pano in taking a government contract to build a house for the "stockman" (veterinary assistant) that the authorities proposed stationing in Bisipara. (All three of them happened to turn up at the same time with suitable gifts—a chicken and rice and lentils—for the allocating official, who accepted the gifts and insisted they take a joint contract or none at all.) In August 1955, when there was a severe drought and the village was raising money to pay for rituals that would bring back the rains, individual Panos willingly contributed. Finally, throughout the troubles, Panos attended major village festivals, as they had always done, without again demanding the right to enter temples.

In short, although one door into the community had been very publicly closed to the Panos, most others remained open. No one, so far as I know, remarked on the inconsistency. Quite possibly the villagers did not see the dismissal of the musicians in the way I did when I first thought about it: as a declaration that deprived the Panos of their membership in Bisipara's moral community. Perhaps that interpretation is too extreme. When we take away privileges—for example, a child's—does that act necessarily disown the child? But the analogy is inept; no kinship is involved between castes. Panos, unquestionably, were of a different essence, a different moral fiber. So was every caste different from every other caste. Nevertheless, despite this perfectly racist sentiment and despite the troubles at that time, there was a strong underlying sense (vague but quite perceptible) that being part of a community was something given, always there, inescapable, a moral inevitability.

Moral inevitability ("truth") is a feature of Gandhian thought, to which I now return.

2

The Way of the Distillers

The Fantasy of Infinite Cooperation

Gandhi's wish was an India that had its essence in its village communities. But this wish was quietly put aside by Nehru and other strong men who guided the Constituent Assembly, which met in Delhi between 1947 and 1949 to put together a constitution for free India. They wanted a modern nation, industrialized, wealthy, and powerful. They respected Gandhi (most of them did), they had ideals, and they were not cynics, but they also saw that their country had to survive in an international world that for the most part was not guided by altruism. Gandhi had a vision, by contrast, of the infinite perfectibility of humankind: human life is a struggle to attain "truth," a moral condition that is part of human nature and that will prevail once obstacles are removed from its way. Our potential for altruism, if only unimpeded, will extend to the very limits of humankind. The impediments are governments and the exercise of power.

Gandhi's world-to-be was founded on humanism. Every person is a worthy person; all action should be voluntary and guided by the golden rule of doing as you would be done by. But it was also a world that rejected individualism, if that word means all men and women pursuing each their own interests. The proper human activity is service to others, to the collectivity, and individuals can only find their "truth" in giving that service, in surrendering themselves to a collectivity in which alone the individual can find truth and fulfillment and therefore—a wonderful paradox—freedom. There are echoes of the corporate state in this design, and, like Mussolini, Gandhi saw no virtue in party politics or in the individual vote; his later devotees spoke derisively of "fifty-one-percent democracy." Unlike Mussolini, however, he saw no virtue in a powerful state or in large organizations of any kind.

In Gandhi's vision the collectivities destined to be the building blocks of the new Indian nation were its villages. B. R. Misra, a later enthusiast and a follower of the Gandhian tradition, put it this hopeful way: "Every village will be the state in itself: the center will have only nominal authority over them. In this way, gradually we will reach the stage when authority in every form will have become unnecessary and will, therefore, fade away giving rise to a perfectly free society" (1956, 56). This would be anarchy in the root sense of the word—a world without rulers—but an amiable anarchy that would not entail disorder. Villagers themselves would find their order, their authentic nature, in the caste system. Individuals would achieve fulfillment of their potentiality in belonging to a caste and doing the work that was its privilege, and castes would be integrated in a village community in the same way that organs are integrated in a body, each making its own particular contribution to the well-being of the whole. Caste, each person following the dharma (which means both doing one's duty and acting in accordance with the natural order of things) was, as Gandhi saw it, a supremely moral system. Untouchability was an aberration to be abolished, but caste was good; it was a natural order, divinely given.

I am sure the people of Bisipara did see caste differences as part of the natural order, a way of sorting people out by natural criteria, not fundamentally different in that respect from distinctions marked by age or sex. Caste was a matter of blood, of genetic inheritance. Many aspects of their daily lives reminded them of differences. Caste separated kin from everyone else; legitimate marriages were all within caste. Caste signalled an order of worthiness, elaborately coded in customs of taking and refusing food. Everyone accepted cooked food from the highest, the Brahmin, and no one but another untouchable would eat from the lowest. Every step on the ladder of worthiness was marked in this way, those above refusing to eat from those below, those below acknowledging their inferiority to those whose food they ate. They also used space to mark separation. The main castes each had their own street in Bisipara, and there was a great fuss from the Distillers when the sirdar, who was the local agent of the government, allotted a garden in the middle of Distiller street (it had fallen to the government in default of heirs) to a Kond client, and the Kond proposed to build himself a house there. I suspect that the sirdar, a Warrior, enjoyed flexing his administrative muscles in that way. Perhaps, also, he was rubbing salt in the wound, for it was said that there had in fact been Distiller heirs, but the headman's predecessor (his father) had so distorted the record that the land escheated to the government, and so came under his control.

Gandhi dismissed the adversarial features of caste and denied outright the premise of different levels of worthiness (he made a public-relations point of eating with untouchables and of requiring everyone in his ashram, irrespective of caste, to take turns at "untouchable" tasks, such as sweeping up rubbish and cleaning toilets). The virtue that he saw in caste was its fundamental assumption that cooperation is the natural mode of social interaction. Each caste works at its own particular task, as nature intends, and so makes its contribution to the whole. A highly simplified model of the caste system in Bisipara presents the Brahmins as priests, the Warriors as owners and managers of the land, and so on. The Herdsmen herd cattle, the Washermen launder clothes, the Barbers cut hair, the Potters make pots, and the untouchables are musicians and weave cloth and dispose of dead cattle. The model assumes cooperation and makes no place for competition or outright conflict. That definitive assumption of harmony found Gandhi's approval. (A few others, notable

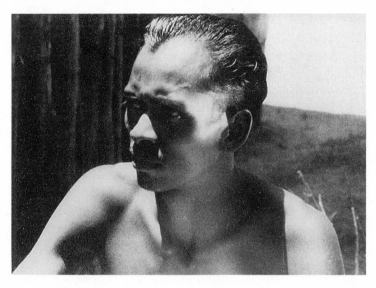

A Warrior, Debohari Bisoi. He was the schoolmaster in the Kond village of Boida.

An elderly Herdsman, whose home was in Phulbani. He was known and respected in Bisipara. He worked as our cook.

among them Dr. Ambedkar, an untouchable to whom I will come
later, spoke openly and forcefully about the other face of caste: it
was a hegemonic invention used by the strong to oppress the
weak.)

The model of a well-adjusted organism that Gandhi saw is
quite far from reality. His vision of infinite altruism is nowhere
realized and is at best no more than a slight mitigation of harsher
motivations. No system that rests on a complex division of labor,
not even small-parcel arrangements like caste in rural India, can
survive for long—or perhaps even come into existence—unless
someone is in charge. Social systems are designs for coping with
a real world that changes of its own accord, and someone with
authority must stand by to adjust the system to the changes that
happen, willy-nilly, in the external world. Managers and guardians are also required to control the human propensity for cheating and thus to counter cheating's product, mistrust. A division
of labor is a continuing bargain that will only work if the part-
ners have reason to trust each other to stick with the bargain.
Certainly conscience (Gandhi's solution) helps to keep the system running, but nowhere is it enough. An external guarantor of
trust—ultimately the state—is the (sometimes unstable) rock on
which a modern industrial economy, anathema to Gandhi, rests.
But in actuality village economies too require (and in fact have) a
partly externalized authority. In Bisipara's model, the Warriors
(not the Brahmins) were that authority. They were the dominant
caste; they had power.

If power were exercised for that purpose alone—seeing that
matters go smoothly and people do their duty—power would
surely be morally acceptable. The problem is, as everyone knows,
that guardians everywhere fall victim to the very temptations
from which they are supposed to guard others: they betray their
trust and seek power for their own advantage instead of using it
for the public interest. That being so, those who are disadvantaged may not perceive altruism in their leaders; instead they
may interpret moralizing about duty as nothing but a hypocritical rhetoric that facilitates exploitation. The elaborate scheme of

caste hierarchy, sorting out the pure from the less pure, is, from this point of view, a tranquilizing device, serving to blunt discontent.

Hinduism explains the present life as the precipitate of conduct in past lives; one's position now represents the balance between merits and demerits accumulated in an earlier existence. Merit, moreover, is acquired not by ambition and seeking a higher status, nor by changing the world to make it better, but by following one's dharma, doing one's duty as a Warrior (guarding the dharma itself), as a Distiller (making liquor), or as a Pano (making music and weaving and scavenging). To aim higher than the present life, to emulate those of superior worthiness, is a sure way to earn demerits. Thus the myths of caste exclude competitive ambition from the natural order of things, since that order itself embodies the "natural" distribution of power. Competition is thereby unrecognized and the field is left clear for cooperation. But, even if proscribed in the mythical charter, competition for power finds its way through the back door and gives the mythology of infinite cooperation a whiff of hypocrisy. Gandhi refused to see the inevitability of that penetration and its resulting corruption.

When we in Western countries talk of power and its distribution, we tend to simplify by going to the two extremes; we see the social world in binary fashion, class-warfare style, as divided irreconcilably and absolutely into just two groups, the overprivileged and the downtrodden. The people of Bisipara did not see their world in that simple way: they made room for greater relativity. Indian intellectuals in the 1950s, contemplating the United States, were fond of remarking that everyone in India belonged to a minority. Bisipara was not two parts, the haves and the have-nots, but a ladder-like arrangement of ritual worthiness and unworthiness ("purity" is the English word generally used): at the top the few Brahmins, then the politically dominant caste of Warriors (a fifth of the population), then the small group of Herdsmen, and beneath all these a variety of others down to untouchables.

Bisipara people accepted this system, intellectually and emotionally, and did not question the premise of inequality. They sometimes questioned their own position on the ladder, and I am sure that all those above the bottom found comfort in contemplating others below them. The prospect of a total revolution, one that did away entirely with hierarchy, they would have found hard to entertain, even hard to imagine. It was much easier for those who resented their present inferiority to think about improving their own position in the scheme of things than to plan a revolution that would abolish the scheme altogether.

Such ambitions violate the primal myth, if the myth is accepted as gospel in all its particulars. But one need not do that; one can accept the principle of hierarchy and at the same time claim that the placings are out of order, having been distorted by other people to further their own ambitions. In that case climbing the ladder is not a violation of the prime directive but a step in the direction of truth, of restoring an order that the guardians had let slip. Notice again that this is not the basic Gandhian notion that all castes are of equal moral worth; it is the reverse.

A central dogma stresses that Brahmins, those who are the most worthy, do *not* exercise secular power. Noticing this, scholars have been tempted into talking about caste at a level of abstraction that separates it entirely from power. But that separation is the Brahmins' version of how the world should work, and it is a claim that neatly upholds their own status as the ultimate arbiters of what the natural order is. Brahmins thus become guardians who cannot themselves be corrupted by power, and their doctrinal authority thus can never be challenged. But that is the world of philosophers, at best of jurists. Communities on the ground, like Bisipara, do not conduct themselves on those principles. Nor does Bisipara's history uphold the notion that control over resources and position in the hierarchy are independent of one another. This is clearly shown in the history of the Distillers of Bisipara.

The Distillers as Social Climbers

In 1870 the liquor shops in the district to the south of the Kondmals, Ganjam (then part of the Madras Presidency), were closed by the administration, and a number of Distillers were deprived of their living. They migrated northwards and joined with local Distillers in pressuring the Kondmals administration (then in the Bengal Presidency) to introduce a ban on home stills. The case no doubt was made on moral grounds—alcoholic excess was best regulated through licensed points of sale—and helped out by the prospect of government revenue derived from the sale of licenses. Seventeen years later there were 470 such licensed outlets in the Kondmals, all of them in the hands of Distillers, both those recently arrived from Ganjam and those, as in the case of Bisipara, from Boad in the north and of long standing in the region. To own a license was, as the licensee of a commercial television station in Britain once said about his enterprise, like having a license to print money.

Between 1887 and 1908 the administration held a series of inquiries into the effects of the out-still system on the Konds. There was a drawn-out contest between Ollenbach, who championed total prohibition, and the liquor interests, who, I assume, were the local Distiller notables. They had evidently mastered the rules of political in-fighting, because they managed to divert attention away from the harm they were inflicting on the Konds by complaining that Ollenbach was a most immoral man and should be removed from office. (He was an Anglo-Indian bachelor, posted to the Kondmals in 1901, and, I suspect, he did not live a celibate life during his more than twenty years among the Konds. A portrait of him, to be seen on the wall of the Phulbani collectorate in 1952, showed a marked resemblance to a middle-aged, pale-complexioned Kond, a cook employed in the collectorate, who bore the nickname Rango, "the colored one.")

Ollenbach had good reason to champion the Konds. Alcoholism apart, they were forfeiting large amounts of land to Distillers. The drink seller's technique was to give credit against the security of a field to a drunken (and illiterate) Kond customer, have his mark on a document witnessed, and eventually foreclose. Some of Bisipara's Distiller families became very rich in that way. Eventually, in 1908 when a Baptist missionary put the issue before a wider public by writing to a Calcutta newspaper, the battle was won for total prohibition, and the Konds went back to making their own liquor, this time probably not in their homes but discreetly somewhere deep in the forest, as they still did in 1953.

I do not know how much land the Distillers owned before 1870. What I heard in Bisipara is that it was an insignificant amount. I do know that in 1953, more than forty years after the liquor shops had shut down, their per capita annual income from land was the same as that of the Warriors, who in the traditional scheme of things were the only legitimate landowners. It seems that, once given a head start through liquor licensing and the out-still system, enterprising Distillers continued to prosper as shopkeepers and traders, and some of them, later, as contractors. Whatever the source of wealth, by the 1950s the modal Distiller household was better off than the modal household of any other caste in Bisipara.

When I began to inquire systematically into the way in which food exchanges were used to signify status in the caste hierarchy, it quickly became clear that the position of the Distillers was ambiguous. Some other parts of the hierarchy were quite clear. Brahmins ate from no one but each other; everyone ate from Brahmins. Panos ate from everyone; no one but Panos ate from Panos. Herdsmen took food from Warriors, but the reverse was not true. Warriors did, however, accept water from Herdsmen, but they did not accept water or food from Distillers. Neither did Herdsmen; neither did Potters. But Distillers, in their turn, would take food and water only from Brahmins. The refusal constitutes a claim to be superior to all the other castes except the Brahmins. The claim was rejected by all clean castes refusing to take food or water from Distillers. A similar ambiguity came to the surface when I asked people to rank castes. Distillers put themselves second only to Brahmins, giving third place to Warriors, then Herdsmen and so on down to Washermen and Weavers, humble castes but not yet in the domain of untouchability. Warriors put Herdsmen below themselves, then Potters, or sometimes Distillers. Herdsmen concurred, putting either Potters or Distillers below themselves. There was, in short, a tendency to place Distillers lower than one's own caste, but not in the lowest segment of the clean-caste hierarchy.

This uncertainty was not especially visible in day-to-day behavior. Even in ritual it was managed quite smoothly. Bisipara people were not in the habit of challenging statuses by thrusting cooked food at one another. Uncooked food for the most part carries no message about relative status, so it became the custom for Warriors to contribute to weddings or funerals in Distiller households by giving the raw materials for a feast. The Distillers reciprocated. When I had been in the village for some time I could detect the signs of the Distillers' arriviste status. Even this was not unambiguous, because the Distillers who came in particularly for snide remarks were those like the elected chairman of the statutory village council, Basu Pradhan, whose ambitions in the world outside the village were transparent enough to make him, almost by definition, an unreliable person.[1] There was, however, a history of needling Distillers when the chance arose, as in the case of the Kond encouraged to build his house in the middle of their neighborhood. Warriors also occasionally made fun of Distiller pretensions to respectability, a manifestation of prejudice that is not to be admired but is also, it should be noticed, the mildest of the three forms of ethnic hostility that I described earlier.

The Distillers were in fact following a modestly successful strategy of ethnic advancement. The procedures for doing this in the context of a caste system, which have often been described, are in flat defiance of the rule of dharma, which prohibits follow-

[1] The statutory village council (*gram panchayat*) was an elected local government body established in 1956. See Chapter 7. It should not be confused with the traditional village council (*panchayat*).

ing any way of life except that of one's own caste. The strategy, surely found in all systems of social stratification, is to emulate the manners and customs of those at the top. In Bisipara, as in the rest of Hindu India, the Brahmins were at the top. The ideal Brahmin was a vegetarian (in fact those in Bisipara were not), so the Distillers proclaimed themselves vegetarian (but mostly continued to eat meat on festive occasions, as did other people). The ideal Brahmin did not drink alcohol, so the Distillers did not drink. (In Bisipara, apart from a few individual topers, only the Panos and the Potters were habitual drinkers.) The respectable Hindu man, whether Brahmin or not, did not send his women to work out in the fields. A few Distiller households lived up to this precept, but most of them could not afford to do without the labor of their womenfolk, especially at paddy-planting time. All such departures into respectability were noticed by the other high castes (they also had an especially sharp eye for the lapses) and treated with a mild, and always discreet, mockery. The discretion, of course, reflects the fact that the Distillers were relatively rich and the rich have clout.

There are other devices for caste climbing, which at the time I did not think about and therefore did not inquire into, although I suspect they were used. These have to do with the *jajmani* system. In the traditional order of things, the Warriors, as landowners, are *jajmans*. Those who do the work for them—Brahmins, Barbers, Herdsmen, and the rest—are *kamins*. They are paid by a customary share of grain given out at threshing time; they also receive food, cooked or uncooked, each time they perform the service. Respectability in the village is partly measured by the ability to command the services of village specialists—in particular the Brahmin, the Barber, and the Washerman—for household rituals. There are two steps in the direction of high status. First, one either receives the services or does not; second, one pays for them either in cash or in the jajmani idiom of a family retainer. The point is that only landowners may qualify for jajmani service; lesser people pay cash; still lesser people do not get the service at all.

The game would have gone like this (I did not actually see it played). The aspirant household would bribe the Barber or Washerman or Brahmin to provide the service, if it had not been provided before, or to switch from cash to the jajmani register, if the service had hitherto been bought. The risk for the service household is that other patrons might object and say that its services are now polluting; or that other households in the service caste will claim that the offender is debasing the coinage and expel him in order to keep their own reputation clean. Unfortunately, I can find no record of how many, if any, of the several Distiller households were served in the mode of jajmani. I do know that none of them were barred from service-for-cash by any of the village specialists. Nor did I hear any stories of them having in the past maneuvered themselves into the position of cash customer. No Pano household was served at all.

All these strategies for social advancement—making a statement in the idiom of food, following the manners and customs that characterize Hindu gentlefolk, or trying to manipulate the jajmani signifiers of respectability—call for a degree of consensus that is not required when social climbing is done in the idiom of class. The newly rich in the ambience of industrial capitalism— or of any type of society that is large enough to feature impersonality and, consequently, measure social standing by conspicuous consumption or some other visible index of status—can leave behind the humbler people among whom they began life, even their own kinfolk. The consent they need to buy is that of the class to which they aspire, not the class they are leaving. It is otherwise in a place like Bisipara, where the rule of dharma gives individuals an ineradicable identity as part of their caste. If status is to be changed, it must be that of the entire group, or at least a sufficiently large part of it, not the status of the ambitious individual alone. Would-be social climbers in a caste system are thus forced into a kind of altruism: if they are going up they must take their kin and their caste fellows along with them. Social climbing, in short, is not done directly by individual effort but by group action. This is for perfectly practical reasons. The lone climber, having cut himself off entirely from his origins, would have no way to get his children married, no means of holding a proper funeral when someone in his family died, and no social life.

Also, it should be remembered, Bisipara is a small place. Even the Kondmals—all of its eight hundred square miles—is a small place. Everyone may not know everyone, but they either know about them or would have no trouble tapping into a reservoir of informative gossip. In the Kondmals there are no circles of root-oblivious well-to-do families such as one finds in the cities of the industrial world. Rootlessness in rural India is generally the penalty inflicted on those few who disgrace themselves and are outcasted. A single wealthy household in Bisipara, newly rich, would have nowhere to go, upwards, if it tried to go alone.

What the Panos Could Not Do

There were seventeen households of Boad Distillers, containing 6.7 percent of the village population. All but a few were well off and, as I remember, none lived in utter poverty. A few worked some of the time as field laborers, but generally for other Distiller households. In other respects too there was a homogeneity among the Distillers that the Panos lacked. Distillers sat astride commerce and cultivation, some more into one than the other, but there was no occupational division within them that produced markedly different lifestyles. For sure, they varied in their involvement with the world outside—Basu Pradhan, the contractor-merchant-shopkeeper-would-be-politician being at one extreme—but the variation was not marked and none of the households would have been considered excessively unsophisticated, on the level, say, at which Konds were stereotyped. The Distillers, in short, were homogenized into a bourgeoislike respectability.

Pano street was quite different. Boad Panos were 21.7 percent of the village population, numbering forty households, and they

Porsu Sahani, a Boad Pano, the senior village watchmen, and a praja of
the Warrior sirdar. He is celebrating the wedding of the sirdar's eldest
son, Jaya Bisoi, who can be seen in the background under the umbrella,
hoisted on the shoulders of one of his father's Kond subjects.

spanned the range from extreme poverty to three or four households that were as rich as the better-off Warriors. At one end was
the household of Sindhu the schoolmaster, who built and offici-
ated in the new Shiva temple; and alongside him was a Congress
constituency agent, an ex-policeman, another man who was an
army pensioner, and, as I remember, another schoolmaster. A
few households prospered buying turmeric in Kond villages and

THE WAY OF THE DISTILLERS

Porsu, on the same occasion, taking over the drums. The man on the right is a Ganjam Pano, one of those who replaced the dismissed Boad Pano musicians.

selling it to merchants in Bisipara or Phulbani. One man made a good living for himself as the priest officiating at the shrine of the deity who controlled smallpox—the deity is Thakurani, whose name might be glossed as "Her Majesty."[2] Three or four household heads were village watchmen, clients of the Warrior sirdar, enjoying both his patronage and the right to cultivate fields allocated by the government. Many households only made ends meet by day labor in fields owned by wealthier persons of another caste. At the bottom end were distinctly jungly people,

[2] In former days certain Pano families had been inoculators. The material used was taken from a person recovering from smallpox. About the turn of the century the practice was forbidden, and efforts were made to replace it with the much safer procedure of vaccination.

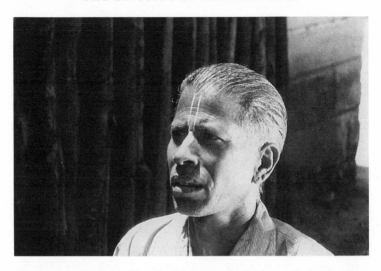

Sindhu Sahani, the well-to-do Pano who built a temple in the Pano street. He was a schoolmaster.

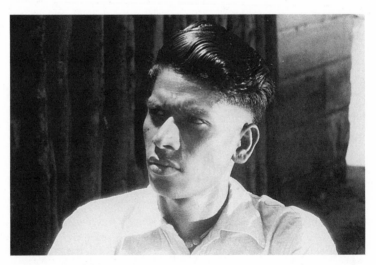

Sindhu's younger brother, Prophulo.

not only illiterate but also drunkards and rowdy and sometimes violent.

In short, the street of the Panos quite lacked the bourgeois homogeneity of the Distillers; its salient feature was variety and, it must be added, it had a boisterous vitality that the Distillers, at least in the 1950s, seemed to lack. (Their community may have been more lively in the days of robbery-by-liquor-license.)

That heterogeneity gets in the way of social climbing, Distiller-style. It is hard to achieve respect in the mode of Hindu piousness—vegetarianism and sobriety—when your own cousins get rowdily drunk on festive occasions and are known to enjoy a meal of beef when someone's cow dies. The very thought of such behavior made clean caste people cynical about self-improving Panos. When they encountered Sindhu—respectable, educated, quiet-spoken, sober, claiming to be a vegetarian, his forehead banded with the painted marks of a Shiva's devotee—they saw him as a Holy Willie putting on the appearance to hide an inner godlessness, in short, as a pretentious fake. (That feeling surely underlies Debohari's vituperative editing of Sindhu's text, quoted earlier.)

The other two strategies also were problematical. No clean caste person would have accepted food from an untouchable, but the Panos could still have taken the halfway step and refused food offered by clean castes, or perhaps have insisted that materials for a feast be given raw, as they were to Distillers or to a Brahmin when he performed a service in one of his jajmani households. But this was not done, so far as I know. Unfortunately it did not occur to me to find out how Sindhu and the rest of the Pano elite conducted themselves on that front, but I do know that many others, typically those who worked for clean-caste households, readily accepted food and water from those they thus acknowledged to be their superiors. As for the service of specialist castes, that was out of the question. Panos could buy certain kinds of status-neutral services—a Brahmin, for example, if paid enough, would read a horoscope for them—but none of the intimate, household-oriented ritual services provided at marriages and funerals were available to them. Any Brahmin (or Washerman or Barber) who did such work would at once have lost his own status, being dismissed by his clean-caste patrons and expelled by his own caste fellows.

The Panos, in short, would have found it difficult to get their act together, as the Distillers did, to make a challenge and take advantage of the flexibility that inhered, dharma notwithstanding, in Bisipara's caste hierarchy. Inasmuch as wealth is the starter, some households (Sindhu's, for example) would certainly have been qualified to make an attempt at social climbing in the Hindu idiom, but many others, the majority, would at best have constituted dead weight, unhelpful because their style of life conspicuously unfitted them for Hindu respectability. Moreover, those Pano households that were not well off were not at all motivated to make the attempt, because they would have paid a heavy cost if their clean-caste employers had taken umbrage enough to sack them and find workers elsewhere.

That difference in wealth might have opened the way, in theory but not in practice, for the better-off Panos to attempt the middle-class root-oblivious strategy. This strategy occurs when a segment of a formerly disadvantaged group finds its way upwards and can form its own enclave, so to speak, within the middle classes. The stereotype of such people is that they abandon those they have left behind, refusing to see any economic or political advantage in identification with them, marrying within their own group and even beginning to exhibit an emotional prejudice against the kind of people from whom they themselves originated. (In the United States militant ethnicity, multiculturalism, and the demise of the melting pot seem to have put an end to that strategy, at least for those blacks who are in the public eye.) This elevation and separation theoretically could occur even in a caste system if a sufficient number of households made the break together. The fact that in the Kondmals several castes, for example Warriors and Distillers, are internally divided into subcastes, and that these subcastes refuse intermarriage, give themselves the appellation "great" (as in "Great Distillers"), and call the other group "lesser" or "unrefined," may be evidence of such splits in the past. I do not know if this was so. In any case the question is moot, because almost all the Bisipara Panos were agnatic kin and could not have formed an in-marrying group, and I heard nothing of classlike connections with status-improving Panos in other Oriya villages in the Kondmals.

The question is doubly moot, because another quite fundamental obstacle stood in the way of "constitutional" advancement: the brute cultural fact of untouchability. The barrier between clean caste and untouchable, in Bisipara minds, had a quality of sacredness, of being absolute and unquestionable, that was not found in the middle reaches of the caste hierarchy and was approached (but not equaled) only at its upper end, in the divide between the Brahmins and the rest. I do not know why Bisipara people saw the world that way, any more than I know why, for example, absolute color distinctions exist in some societies but not in others, or why black hair does not constitute a mark of disqualification in the way that a black skin does. But Bisipara people did frame untouchability as an unquestionable moral imperative. When Distillers, who were not untouchables, became rich, they were able to work within a set of pragmatic rules to elevate themselves in the caste hierarchy without other people seeing their actions as a revolutionary obscenity. I cannot imagine a similar accommodation being made for Panos, even if they had all been as rich and as bourgeois as the Distillers. Too many deeply internalized "truths" would have had to be unlearned. At least it would have taken more time.

The Panos, as I said, were not all rich, and they were not homogenized into respectability, as the Distillers were. But some were rich enough to follow a style of life that, in the case of a clean-caste person, could only have been considered respectable. The Panos had a vanguard, not an intelligentsia but rather an elite of sophisticated activists, who, predictably, were rich enough to resent being slighted. But even this elite did not speak with one voice or see their world and its possibilities in the same way, being divided between those who were militant and those who were, so to speak, constitutionalists.

The division parallels one found earlier in the movement for

Indian independence, between those who believed in round-table talking and those who took direct action. The former put their trust in the rationality and ultimate good intentions of the British, their willingness to grant Indians self-rule through a process of negotiation and civilized discussion. The round-table people dominated and guided the Congress movement from its inception in 1885 until after the turn of the century. Then, in Bengal and Maharashtra, terrorists and assassins demonstrated that there were cruder and more direct ways to press for nationhood. Early in the 1920s Gandhi emerged with a third strategy, nonviolent but subordinating quasi-judicial reasoning to an impassioned morality. Gandhi's way prevailed and, as I said, was still in the 1950s the respectable, and often effective, device for turning up the heat under those in power.

The Pano "Freedom Fight" in Bisipara (to make the episode a bigger deal than in fact it was) had no equivalent of the bomb-throwers and assassins. It did have, however, a few "constitutionalists," people such as Sindhu, who seemed to believe that respect could be won within the framework of Hinduism and that the way used by the Distillers would be open also for Panos; or at least it was worth a try. The other set of Panos went along with the attempt—none of them seemed entirely to be of one mind—but later decided that this particular route was closed. The better way forward was to go around the obstacle of the village community and move outwards to a larger polity altogether, one that lay ideologically beyond Hinduism. Toward the end of the 1950s large numbers of untouchables in northern and western India converted to Buddhism. The quasi-militant wing of the Bisipara Panos remained Hindu but subordinated their religious status and selected, as their essential strategic attribute, citizenship.

I never heard the Pano elite discuss the issue, and I have deduced the two strategies from the actions they took. The event that started.my train of thought was a non-event, tactics that the Panos chose not to follow. They set out on the quasi-militant path of confrontation, but then they stopped. Having taken the trouble to confront the Warriors with the Temple Entry Act, and having taken the additional risk of making sure that the authorities knew what was going on, why did they not follow through? Why did they not make the attempt again at other festivals or at the same festival in later years? Why did they not follow the suggestion that I imagine the sub-inspector must have made and immediately take their case to court? Most of all, what is signified, not only by this inaction, this apparent retreat, but also by building the Shiva temple in their own street?

Some of those questions have immediate plausible answers, although I do not know how close they come to the facts. Making a case in court is expensive, time-consuming, and surely with an uncertain outcome, constitutional rights notwithstanding, when the plaintiffs are Panos who have a reputation for being troublemakers. As for staging further confrontations at a temple, if they had done so they would probably have risked violence and punitive action by the police. Violence would also have been, as I have suggested, out of tune with the image that Panos were trying to create for themselves, which was the Gandhian mode of nonviolent reasonableness-fronting-for-obstinacy. In other words, they were packaging themselves as Harijans.

Building the Shiva shrine in Pano street probably did several things. Some Panos may have seen it as quite practical and only incidentally, if at all, symbolic: it provided a place where they could fulfill their own spiritual needs. Sindhu could well have been of this mind. But the act also sent a variety of messages to those able or willing to hear. First, it was a testimony to Hindu piousness, a small foothold in the domain of that religion's respectability, analogous to the Distillers' conspicuous refusal to drink alcohol or eat meat. If that was a message intended for the clean castes, I never heard it acknowledged. Second, in part it could have been a message to the Panos themselves from Sindhu and others who thought as he did, that Hinduism offered them salvation. The implications of this are wholly Gandhian, in effect asserting that devotion alone will suffice, that all are equal before the divinity. In fact, of course, this would have to be the case:

there could be no untouchability where all the congregation were untouchables. Hierarchy was thus banished from the Shiva temple in Pano street more effectively than in Gandhi's own multicaste scheme: there is no caste hierarchy where there is only one caste.

That message—that all are equal in Shiva's temple—shades into another: the Bisipara Panos are no longer part of the Bisipara community. At least on the spiritual front, they can look after themselves, and they are a separate, independent, and therefore equal community alongside Bisipara's clean castes. The Gandhian version of caste, since it has in it no invidious distinctions of hierarchy, provides the required ideology and authenticates the strategy.

But there are obvious frailties in this scheme. Only to a limited extent could a community be what it claimed to be, when that claim defied a reality that all (including most Panos) accepted. Both economically and on the level of social relationships generally, the Panos were not a separate community. Between Pano households and households across the barrier there was an elaborate network of interdependency. Sindhu was well off and did not depend on any clean-caste household for his living, but he too had friends among the clean castes; he belonged to the informal freemasonry of schoolteachers; and he, along with other leading Panos, actively involved himself in certain matters that concerned the entire village (I will come to them later). In short, the symbolic assertion of an independent and equal Pano community went along with a tacit acknowledgement, from both sides, that the claim to spiritual equality did not entail other kinds of equality. Otherwise there would have been Panos without work and would-be employers without workers.

That shades into another message, a more radical one, that can be derived from the separate Shiva temple. This message claims that Bisipara is no longer a political theater where the performances matter. On a bigger stage a different kind of drama is being presented, and an effective performance on this larger stage will automatically qualify the performers for the higher status that was denied them in the village theater. Consequently, from this point of view, it would have been a waste of time for Panos to exert themselves further over matters like temple entry. Hinduism, as practised by the pragmatists of Bisipara, could serve Distiller ambitions well enough and to some extent give them the dignity that their wealth merited. Ambitious Panos had to find a different strategy.

That mildly revolutionary perception of Bisipara's place in the larger social and political world was realistic. A new kind of political contest, played out in an arena beyond the village, had begun. To varying degrees the emerging situation was seen as regrettable or desirable, or, on another dimension, as a change that still could be held in check, or else as something inevitable. There were ambitious Panos seeking places for themselves in the new world, and they had opponents among the clean castes. But for no one, neither Pano nor clean-caste, was this vision the dominant reality to which all other considerations must be adjusted. The ultimate directive—what really mattered to them—was shaped by quite other values and perceptions.

3

Calculated Restraint

What Was the Goal?

The Pano strategy of confrontation at the temple will seem familiar to anyone who followed the nearly contemporaneous civil rights movement in the United States (which also, through the person of Martin Luther King, derived inspiration from Gandhi). Perhaps what the Panos were doing was what Rosa Parks turned out to have done in Montgomery in 1955 when she refused to give up her seat on the bus, or what other blacks did in the southern states when they seated themselves at lunch counters reserved for whites. Flags were being hoisted. Although the word would have seemed bizarre in India in the 1950s, the Panos were attempting to "integrate" the Shiva temple. I am sure this was the case. But what "civil rights" they hoped to gain by doing so is a more complicated question. Temple entry was a prize in itself, but it was also, perhaps, a key to other rights. It is unclear, though, what price they were willing to pay.

What is clear, as I think back and set the temple entry agitation against civil rights campaigners in the United States, is a marked lack of impassioned behavior in Bisipara and a fondness for short-run cost-benefit calculation. No one in Bisipara, Pano or clean-caste, was sufficiently secure economically or sufficiently desperate to act in disregard of the short-run consequences. (I am sure there were prudent calculators among the blacks of the American South, too. But that attitude went mostly unheeded by the media and so was unreported.) One reason for this persistent caution, as will become clear later, was the relatively closed structure of Bisipara's community. There were no Freedom Rides to Bisipara and no significant number of outsiders passionately committed to the Pano cause. (In fact, there was only one outsider active in that way, a semi-official person, dutiful but hardly impassioned. More on him later.)

When one asks what the Panos hoped to gain at the Sibhomundiro, there is an array of possible answers. That type of challenge—temple entry or access to lunch counters—may be issued solely to make a claim about status, addressing only dignity, and seemingly centered on nothing but the intangible quality of identity. The challenger wants recognition as a moral person, as a justified recipient of the benefits implied in "Do unto others as you would be done by."

But, as I noted earlier, that may not have been the primary motive; it may not even have been a motive at all. Status may have been an unconsidered by-product. Observers who are accustomed to seeing the world as discourse slip comfortably into an interpretive mode that sees only symbols and is blind to everything else. They are alert to gas, but never think there might be solids too. In their view it's not the hamburger that the civil rights activist wants at the lunch counter but only the right to eat there. Now, in the case of the lunch counter sit-in, that interpretation surely is correct. But one can hunger for food as well as for status, and no one can deny that in the last resort food comes first. Rosa Parks turned out to be a militant message-sender, but she began as someone tired, wanting to stay in her seat. In the same way at least some Panos may have seen access to the Shiva temple as a practical benefit, an instrumental necessity, irrespective of any message it might carry about status. Think of the Shiva temple as a clinic or a college or anything else wanted for its utility. The deity has practical spiritual benefits to confer. The Panos' new temple, built in their own street for their own exclusive use, fits well with that line of reasoning.

Putting that question aside, and imagining the confrontation only as a statement about identity, it is not at all clear where Panos drew the boundaries. What identities did they want involved in the situation? There are many possibilities. At first sight the confrontation was about untouchability itself, and therefore centered on the domain of Hinduism. The message was: This particular mark of disadvantage—limited access to temples—is no longer an acceptable feature of Hinduism. But other matters could have been involved. Along with limited access to temples goes limited access to other people's persons, to their houses, to wells, to the meeting house, and so forth. Removing all those indicators of inferiority was part of the Harijan package. Was that aspiration or threat (it depends on whose side is taken) part of anyone's agenda in Bisipara? Was access to the temple a first step in the direction not only of ritual homogeneity but also of "monoethnic" equality? The latter would have involved intermarriage, and, I am sure, no one's imagination went that far.

Second, there were other more immediate consequences, at least as possibilities. In places like Bisipara untouchability also entailed (by the 1950s somewhat approximately) a particular place in the organization of production. As I have explained, Panos were prajas, which in its economic aspect meant that they were agricultural laborers. Many more of them were day laborers (*mulya*), and the village economy could not have functioned without them. That, as will become clear, is another complicating factor. From one side, it set a limit on the arena of confrontation; most people did not want to risk deprivation just to make a point about relative dignity. Alternatively, those Panos who were now rich had already won their economic battle; for them temple entry was no more than a bid for symbolic recognition of their victory.

Third, despite the venue, the message may have had nothing much to do directly with the Hindu religion; it may have been, as I said earlier, an attempt to assert citizenship and demonstrate that power in the village was becoming a secondary matter, because the real prizes were to be won in the arena of local and state political institutions. The so-called statutory panchayat, a new form of elective local government, was coming into being at that time. Statewide political parties had (somewhat embryonic) organizations in the region, and—a real novelty—it was beginning to dawn on some villagers that officials were answerable not just to higher officials but also to elected politicians. The logical end of this, however—the idea that all these people, officials and representatives alike, were the servants of the people—was not part of the image that people in Bisipara had of the raj, their government.

All these issues will have a hearing. Let me begin by considering the venue of the confrontation and its significance. Since the contexts of discrimination were many, so also were the theaters, both religious and secular, where a challenge against untouchability might be staged. The Panos, no doubt prompted by the Temple Entry Act, chose to do so at a temple, and at a particular temple. Out of the three available, they chose the Sibhomundiro.

Why Shiva's Temple?

Why that temple? I do not know for sure, because I have no record of the discussions the Panos must have held before they took action. Obviously a decision was made and the challenge at the temple was not a spontaneous spur-of-the-moment affair. If it had been, they could not have made their intentions known beforehand both to the Warriors and to the authorities. But I do not know who among them took the lead on this occasion, nor what reasons were advanced for making the confrontation at the Shiva temple instead of the little-used temple in Market street or Sri Ramchandro's "house" in Warrior street. Nevertheless, it is instructive to work out the costs and benefits of choosing one or another of the three possible sites for the confrontation, not with the idea of calculating a "bottom line" and implying that this was precisely how the Panos reasoned things out, but in order to see what meanings inhere in each of the three possibilities. All three would carry the message of a challenge and a protest, but in each case there are other and different messages packed into the rhetorical bundle.

Of the three temples, the one in Market street was the least significant. It had been built by Chano Mehera, the Weaver, who had prospered in trade and money lending. Later, when his life began to fall apart, experts he consulted told him that the resident deity was unhappy and advised him to pay to have it removed to the town of Puri. The Weaver did so, at great expense to himself and some profit to the experts, but his decline continued, and eventually the Bisipara panchayat took over management of the temple. In 1953 they were using it to store Sri Ramchandro's sacred paraphernalia while Sri Ramchandro's own house in Warrior street was being rebuilt. Minimal daily rituals were performed in the Market street temple, but there were no major festivals similar to those that took place at the Shiva temple or at Sri Ramchandro's temple, when all the village, clean castes and untouchables alike, attended to make their offerings. For this reason the Market street temple would not have been a good place for a confrontation: it did not offer a suitable audience and the right publicity.

In that respect Sri Ramchandro's temple would have been very suitable; it was, so to speak, media-appropriate. In particular, each year at the end of March and the beginning of April there was a two-week festival, which everyone in the village attended, culminating in a hugely theatrical occasion, the burning of Ravana's palace, which brought in a thousand or more people from villages all around. (The festival was even noticed in the tourist section of a handbook put out by the Orissa government's Public Relations Department.) This grand spectacle itself would not have been tactically appropriate for a temple entry confrontation, since it took place in the open fields at the northern edge of the village, well away from Sri Ramchandro's temple in Warrior street. Where the crowds assembled there was no temple to be entered and therefore no place suitable for making the challenge. But there was such an occasion earlier in the festival; it was not attended, it is true, by the huge crowds of the palace-burning day, but at least everyone in the village was present. On the opening afternoon of Sri Ramchandro's festival all the people in the village came to his temple bearing offerings, exactly as they did later in the year at the Shiva temple. I saw it done in 1953; on that occasion the Panos too brought their offerings and made their obeisances, but there was no demonstration and they made no attempt to enter the sacred enclosure, as the women and men of clean caste freely did.

To have done so would have had consequences significantly different from what took place after the Panos asserted their legal right to enter the Sibhomundiro. Ramchandro's house belonged clearly and unambiguously to Bisipara in a way that the Shiva temple did not. There was a clear sense in which the Ramchandro temple, unlike the Shiva temple, *personified* Bisipara. The temple and the people were, to use a Christian idiom, of the one body. More prosaically, Ramchandro's house achieved a level of sacredness for Bisipara people that they did not grant the Shiva temple, even though it, too, was located in Bisipara, was managed by Bisipara people, and Bisipara people worshipped there.

This fact has several entailments. First, the Ramchandro temple was parochial; it focused the loyalties of Bisipara people; it was *their* concern and not the concern of outsiders. If the Panos had made their challenge there, they would have localized the confrontation. But the Shiva temple belonged to "all the people of the Kondmals." At first thought, the costs of using that temple to make the confrontation might have outweighed the benefits, because it would have increased the size of the opposition and made it easier for the Warriors and the other clean castes to mobilize support across the region. On the other hand, it is a common feature of protest movements that outrageous behavior, even if it causes anger and disgust among those who observe it, at least catches their attention; it administers a psychological

shock. Such conduct is often dismissed as adolescent or immature or neurotic or even branded as criminal. But it may cause
some of those who witness it to examine their consciences and
ask what can be so wrong with things as they are that people are
driven to such extremes. The audience may also be intimidated
by the spectacle of people clearly willing to go beyond the normal rules of civilized behavior. Whatever the reaction, more people are made aware of the grievance, because outrageousness
catches a wider audience than does decorous behavior. In short,
the choice of the Shiva temple for the locus of confrontation, because it potentially involved a larger congregation, brought with
it message-sending advantages of the kind that nowadays cause
television crews to be welcomed more by agitators than by authorities.

Second, confrontation at the Shiva temple left open a door for
compromise and relatively orderly negotiation. That door probably would have been closed if the Panos had tried to force their
way into Sri Ramchandro's temple. Sri Ramchandro's temple
was, as I said, the soul of Bisipara and the seat of its identity (or
at least one of the seats). To violate it would have been to violate
the dignity of the clean castes, primarily the Warriors, in a nota-
bly outrageous fashion, one that could be neither ignored nor
even compromised. Warrior honor (*mohoto*) would be put at risk,
and consequently Warrior reaction would likely have been less
rational and more impassioned. The chances of a violent response would have been much increased. The Sibhomundiro, by
contrast, was only at the margins of the community's self-respect.

Indeed, that is exactly how the affair turned out. The Warrior
response to the sub-inspector was the suggestion (obviously im-
practical, but ostensibly in the spirit of compromise) that he poll
all the Hindus in the Kondmals for their opinion, coupled with a
tongue-in-cheek undertaking to go along with the majority vote.
At least the *form* of the response suggested reasonableness and a
willingness to follow rational, non-violent procedures in order to
negotiate an agreement.

Why should the Panos have been reluctant to risk violence? Why were they careful not to box the Warriors into a position from which violence would have been a likely way of escape? The question suggests itself particularly because violence and disorder, like the outrageous behavior that I mentioned earlier, attract attention. (I recall a conversation in 1959 with an over-sophisticated young Indian politician, then far to the left but when I next met him, twenty years later, a minister in a right-wing government. He told me about the best techniques for provoking a police "firing" so that there would be a martyr or two for the cause.) A reasonable explanation for Pano restraint is that violence would have attracted the wrong kind of attention from people who mattered. The "wrong kind of attention" is easily defined: its costs exceed its benefits. But who are the people whose attention mattered? That question packages a complexity, both at the local and the state level.

One complicating variable I have already mentioned. Who gets the benefits and who pays the costs? Violence might in the long run have been a net plus for the Pano cause, defined simply as an acknowledged right to enter the Shiva temple. But it would have surely involved a heavy short-run (and perhaps long-run) cost for at least some individual Panos. I am not referring to broken heads and houses burned, as happens even now with regrettable frequency in some parts of India. That kind of violence was not a feature of Bisipara's treatment of its untouchables. I mean only that some Panos might have gone hungry, and some clean-caste people might have found it difficult to work their farms. A large number of Panos depended on employment by clean-caste households, and those households reciprocally needed Pano labor to work their fields. Both parties were well aware of this mutual dependence, and I am sure that individuals on both sides knew they would be hurt if they went entirely back-to-back, putting an end to all transactions between them. (Individual and group interests often do not go in tandem. I will consider that interface again later, for it is a key to understanding what went on in Bisipara in those years.)

Thus one audience to be factored into Pano plans for confrontation was the clean-caste population of Bisipara. For the Panos, one right outcome would have been to intimidate the Warriors and their allies enough to make them conform with the Temple Entry Act, but not so much as to disrupt the economic exchanges on which both parties depended. Another audience was the government, a category which until recently in the Kondmals had included only officials; by 1952 there were also some politicians. All but a few people in Bisipara had still to perceive the potential empowerment they might derive, as individuals or groups, from the new notion of government as the servant of the people. For most of them the raj (at least its benevolent side) was still seen in the analogy of mother and father, a combined source of discipline, order, and nurturance; in that metaphor the people have the lower status and are the dependents of the government, not the other way around.

A few Panos—an elite that I will examine more closely later—had got the message that elected representatives, and indeed the very notion of parliamentary institutions and their control over the executive branch of government, offered a new way to manipulate police and revenue officials and various other hitherto seemingly all-powerful figures. The new way was more open and much more adversarial than the traditional mixture of bribery, deception, subservience, and flattery. It required new kinds of political skills, one of which was the ability to use a rhetorical style that was not yet common in places like the Kondmals. Everyone, whether enlightened or not in the ways of the new democracy, whether clean-caste or untouchable, knew very well that manipulation of government had to be done in the appropriate idiom. There was one language, for example, to offer a bribe and another to cajole and flatter. There were also tried and trusted ways of practicing deceit. What was new for the Kondmals was *public* manipulation of authority—open and forceful persuasion as distinct from doing a deal, usually one-on-one and always behind the scenes. Such public challenges could only be made by those who occupied the moral high ground, and they called for the use of an idiom that was morally respectable. In the 1950s the idiom of choice was Gandhian. Gandhi's political strategies relied on relentless moral pressure exerted through non-violent confrontation. That was clearly the politically correct idiom for the Panos. Besides, when it came to temple entry rights, in theory at least they had the law on their side.

In practice the matter was not so clear-cut. The administrators who upheld the law, although officially on no one's side, unofficially had a softer spot for clean castes than they did for Panos. There was still a trace—no more than that—of the nineteenth-century perception of the honest husbandman, which in the Kondmals meant Konds and Warriors. More significant was the negative perception they had of Panos. Everyone, administrators and villagers, had fallen into the habit of seeing criminal tendencies among Panos, and sometimes even the Panos themselves thought that way. They were not formally classified as a "criminal tribe," as had been some castes elsewhere in India, but local administrators lined up with ordinary people in the Kondmals in assuming that Panos were thieves and cheats and troublemakers. Sindhu's text, quoted earlier, allegorizes the situation: Panos were disadvantaged because they supposedly had no land to cultivate and were forced to beg for their food, and so they went hungry, and so they stole, and so they went to jail, until the raj, in the person of A. J. Ollenbach, saved them by giving them land and teaching them how to look after themselves. Ollenbach served in the Kondmals between 1901 and 1924. Nevertheless, still in 1953, Bisipara's Pano street was flagged as a crime spot on a map that I saw in the police station in Phulbani. This being so, it made good sense for the Panos to present their political case in the most respectable manner open to them, which was direct action of the Gandhian non-violent type. The strategy would not have made the police happy—no form of agitation does anywhere in the world—but at least it gave them less excuse to act on the prejudices they already had.

There were other kinds of ambivalence. Ethnic distinctions in Bisipara's traditional scheme of things did not always and irrevocably involve thoroughgoing prejudice. That can also be the case in other societies. In certain situations, even in the ambience of racism, we choose to see only the individual and overlook the ethnic category. There is a legendary American blue-collar "native" (Archie Bunker type), once found in places where urban sociologists work, who is totally prejudiced against blacks but readily consorts with a black individual because he perceives him *as* an individual—"He's Joe." That did not happen much in Bisipara, so far as I could see. People did not fraternize across the line of untouchability, although they did, in the raja-praja relationship, "paternalize." Nor did they entirely submerge the individual in the ethnic category. Most of the time they were quite dispassionate about the whole matter. Everyone knew that not just individual Panos but Panos collectively—Panos ex officio, so to speak—were unredeemably unclean. But it was nothing to be angry about; that was the nature of things, that was their dharma. What mattered, in the case of untouchable prajas or day laborers, was how well they did their work. In other words, individual Panos had some attributes that were independent of the quality of being an untouchable.

Harijan politics promised to change all that. Harijan status began to encroach on other kinds of individual identity. It became harder for clean castes to be dispassionate about a praja or a day laborer, even harder to see any merit in the kind of life that Sindhu lived, a life that they might have admired had Sindhu not been a Harijan. Politicians, administrators, and villagers too, being forced (increasingly, if still only marginally in places like Bisipara) to familiarize themselves with the concept Harijan, lost some of their dispassion. They became angry and were ready to blame Panos for being Harijans, because Harijan was not part of dharma but a status that defied dharma. The situation was all the more confusing and frustrating because Gandhi's campaign made it increasingly hard to keep the stereotype of essential untouchability intact and to see it as unambiguously negative. It was certainly harder to talk openly in those terms.

Violence, providing it could be laid at the door of the Panos (even if they themselves had not used it), would have been at variance with the Harijan image. In the grammar of confrontation used by the Panos, violence would have been a howler, confusing and therefore counterproductive. It might also have brought about immediate and unpleasant consequences. In that region, at that time, although parliamentary institutions and the ethos that goes with them were in the process of creation (in the Kondmals everyone voted for the first time in the winter of 1951–52), the spirit abroad was still that of the authoritarian bureaucracy that the British had created. Nor had that particular region been much affected by the anti-authoritarian tendencies of the "Freedom Fight," as the struggle for Indian independence was then called. People knew about the right to petition a higher official against the excesses of lesser officials, and they knew how to use bribery to protect or to advantage themselves. But they mostly expected officials to be autocratic, swift to act, and—a source of peril for ordinary people—easily made impatient when circumstances were complicated enough to make immediate action difficult. The temple entry incident in Bisipara was complicated. The law was clearly in favor of the Panos. But the Panos were notoriously bad citizens. Moreover, the administrators' nightmare—a breakdown of law and order—seemed at least a possibility.

All those complications would have been swiftly brushed aside by the police if either party had in fact resorted to violence. Violence would have removed the complexity, leaving the police with the straightforward task of using violence to end violence. I think both parties—Panos and Warriors—factored this possibility into their calculations and planned not to give the police the easy option of cracking heads. Short of this extreme, the subinspector's threat (as I imagined it) to billet a couple of constables on the village would have carried the same message: it would be a tactical error to give the police an excuse to act out their inbuilt, unthinking anger.

What Was the Arena?

Since the Panos wanted to avoid violence (I am assuming), the choice of the Shiva temple as the venue for a challenge was perfectly rational. The temple's marginal status in Bisipara made its threatened desecration a less explosive issue, and therefore predisposed the Warriors towards negotiation. The choice of that temple was rational for other reasons too. It was not under the management of the state agency charged with overseeing religious institutions, but in village folklore it was a government institution. Had it not been built by Dinobandu Tahsildar? The Shiva temple, in the eyes of Bisipara people, belonged to a wider world beyond the village, and as such it had to be included within the purview of the Temple Entry Act. The Panos claimed this was so, and the Warriors acknowledged the claim. The act gave the Panos the right to enter the temple, not as residents of Bisipara or as members of its community but as citizens of the state. The state, in this affair, was by its own laws compelled to be their patron and their ally.

To enlist the support of superior allies was not a new tactic in Kondmals politics. From the days of Macpherson to the period I lived in Bisipara, and no doubt still at the present time, powerful individuals curried favor with powerful officials, sometimes even managing to play one off against another. Macpherson's periods of service in the Kond hills alternated with those of the other Scot, Captain (eventually General) Campbell, who, to judge from his writings, was an obtuse and obnoxious man. As one reads their memoirs of the Meriah Wars, the various government reports, and the one-sided and distinctly malicious booklet that Campbell caused to be published about his own achievements and Macpherson's lack of achievement (*Khond Agency* 1849), it becomes obvious from all these sources that some astute local leaders, particularly one "Sam Bissye" (Syamo Bisoi), were using Campbell and Macpherson as patrons to enhance their power in the Kond hills.

That ax-grinding was done in the 1840s. Some time in the first two decades of the nineteenth century, according to the tale told me by the people of Boida (a Kond village near Bisipara), that same Ollenbach became the unwitting strong-arm for one of their more recent ancestors, who used his position as Ollenbach's favorite to amass a huge estate at the expense of his fellow villagers. His name was Dinarosingh Kohoro.

None of this is a surprise. The default mode of government that the British used throughout India was indirect rule. Indigenous governmental institutions were left intact, whenever possible, as a matter of principle. It was also expedient to do so, since changes cause disturbances and disturbances are costly. Customs or institutions that seemed beyond the bounds of "good government and natural justice," such as widow burning, the practice of thuggee (ritual murder), or, in the Kondmals, human sacrifice and female infanticide, were suppressed. Vast changes also were brought about by major country-wide innovations, such as building railways or establishing universities. But in a region like the Kondmals, the primary charge to the administrator was to maintain law and order, collect the revenue, and beyond that let things mostly alone. Some individual officials had their hobbies. Ollenbach, so far as I know the only senior administrator to make himself fluent in the Kond language, made education his specialty, and a surprising number of middle-aged men in Bisipara could read and write (not that they did much) because when they were children Ollenbach used to descend on villages that had schools, call the roll, and fine parents whose children were not in attendance.

Indirect rule in practice requires a person in Ollenbach's position to develop a network of clients among local notables. The result was that informal interactions, as well as the formal apparatus of indirect rule, served to maintain intact the indigenous hierarchy and the existing structure of advantage and deprivation. The superior power represented by the British and their bureaucracy became available to those who were not privileged in the existing system, who were not notables, only when that system fell into disarray. That, I conjecture, must be the story that lies behind the allegory of how Ollenbach came to the rescue of the Panos and gave them land; he had discovered, he must have thought, an enlightened way to solve a law and order problem. But in general Panos could enlist the power of government on their side only piecemeal, at a low level, through bribery. In the courts individual Panos theoretically stood as equals, as citizens, but that status was no remedy for their collective disqualification from the privileges that clean castes enjoyed. In short, until 1947, when the British left India and representative democracy was introduced in the Kondmals, the Panos of Bisipara had no formal ally in government on whom they could call collectively and as of right.

That they, collectively, had acquired such an ally in government was not immediately obvious in the years following Indian independence. The situation, indeed, was filled with contradictions and ambiguities. A main architect of the constitution that emerged out of the 1947–49 deliberations was a lawyer and politician, Dr. Ambedkar, who was himself an untouchable. Ambedkar, who considered Gandhi a hypocrite, found himself caught in an angry debate with a group of politicians who were determined to model the constitution on Gandhian principles, one of which, as I explained, was that the village community must be the fundamental building block of the new polity. The alternative model, favored by Nehru and most of the nation's leaders and championed by Dr. Ambedkar, was a nation state founded on the rights of the individual, one person one vote. "What is the village," he asked, in a ferocious outburst, "but a sink of localism, a den of ignorance, narrow-mindedness and communalism?"[1] ("Communalism" in India means, as I said earlier, religious or ethnic prejudice and strife.) Ambedkar's policy prevailed and India emerged into freedom, constitutionally at least, as a liberal democracy (with socialist tendencies) rather than as a territorial version of the Italian fascist corporate state.

[1] AVARD 1962, 24–25. AVARD is an acronym for the Association of Voluntary Agencies for Rural Development, an organization working to realize the Gandhian model of a decentralized village-based Indian polity.

But India also emerged with a clear recognition that certain categories of people in the new nation were severely disadvantaged. These were the tribals (such as the Konds), formally designated "Scheduled Tribes" and generally referred to as "Adibasis," and the untouchables, formally "Scheduled Castes," and then, after Gandhi's intervention and (an irony) often in the context of political strife, called "Harijans." In the new India both these categories were privileged. They had reserved seats in state assemblies and in the national parliament, they were given privileged access to jobs in the administration and the police, and they benefited from certain other preferential allocations, for example through scholarships and quota systems in institutions of higher education. Thus India went the way of other countries coping with a legacy of past discrimination and was caught in the bind of creating long-run equal opportunity for all by legislating present short-run inequality. The term "short-run" suggests the intention better than the actuality. More than forty years later, the "affirmative action" issue is still a matter of contention and the cause of periodic outbursts of violence in India.

The practice of discrimination in the idiom of untouchability was, in accordance with Gandhi's wishes, made illegal; the various Temple Entry Acts (in existence in some states even before 1947) were part of that legislation. But acts of that kind, initiated from on high, had little effect in places like Bisipara. At that time there were no radios and no television sets in the village, and although a number of the men could read and write, no one regularly read a newspaper. (As I recall, only one woman was literate in 1953. She was the sirdar's young daughter-in-law.) Local officials did not have the manpower—nor very much the will—to go out and, unprompted by events, enforce the new legislation.

But some small effort was made. There did appear in Bisipara, about that time, a touring social worker, possibly a follower of Vinoba Bhave (more on him in Chapter 6), who came to the village and lectured the people. He told them they should give a fifth of their land to the untouchables and warned them that the very use of the word "untouchable" was now a crime. The villagers knew him as the "Harijan inspector" (using the English noun) and behind his back said that their Panos ought to give a fifth of their land to others in the village, because Panos were rich enough to do that. But in fact their defiance was *sotto voce*, and they were intimidated by the inspector's two visits. He was a Fisherman by caste, and, the villagers noticed, he spent a lot of time in prayer. They also remarked that no one ever saw him actually touch a Pano. Here is a description of his second visit, written by Debohari.

For two days in January 1955 the Inspector of Depressed Castes was present in the village. He held a meeting for all Harijans in the Boida ashram school. He wished to hold a meeting in Bisipara on January 13, but both the appropriate presiding officials, the sirdar and the village headman [another Warrior, the sirdar's paternal cousin] happened to be absent at that time.

He came back on January 21 and requested the headmaster of the Bisipara Upper Primary school to convene a meeting in the street of the Warriors. About fifty people were present. Speeches were made by the headmaster [a Brahmin], by a schoolmaster from Gonjagura [a Distiller], by Balunki Sahani [a Bisipara Pano, an agent for the Congress party], and by Sindhu Sahani [the man who wrote the text quoted earlier, also a Bisipara Pano, a schoolmaster]. The Harijan inspector had this to say: "I have heard and I have seen that you Oriyas forbid the Harijans from going into the temple and taking water from the wells." So Dino Bisoi interrupted him and said, "Aren't there wells in every street? Do they ever come to get water here? Would we forbid them if they did? What would be the point? It is their own wish not to come here." Then the Inspector said, "I tell you seriously, if anyone of you forbids them on the grounds of being untouchable, you will be fined five hundred rupees and go to jail for six months."

After that everyone was afraid to say anything, and the meeting broke up.

The villagers were never openly defiant. Usually they offered would-be commonsensical reasons, such as those given by Dino above, why they should continue not to have bodily contact with

Panos. In settings that could be culturally defined as not subject to their own rules and customs, they more or less yielded to the new style. The well that our household used was sircar, "government," and open to anyone. The Bisipara headmaster, in the context of the school, ignored untouchability. All the children sat together. Away from school he behaved like anyone else. In November 1954 a "Basic Training" conference was held in the Bisipara school, attended by schoolmasters, some of whom were Panos. On the final day of the course a feast was given, cooked by the conferees. A government official attended and invitations were sent to leading people in Bisipara, the two sirdars, all the schoolmasters, the merchant-shopkeeper, and some other people. All but one, a Distiller, went to the feast. The Distiller objected to the dining arrangements. The convention was for each caste to sit in a separate line, apart from the others, but on this occasion all were to sit down together in a single line, regardless of caste. (But, Debohari was careful to note, the Panos who attended the course helped with the preparations but did not actually cook the food. Nor, one supposes, were they tactless enough to make a fuss about not being invited to do so.)

Over the years, the Harijan issue in Bisipara slowly became politicized. It did not do so in response to the efforts of the Harijan inspector—at least not primarily. The main reason, I think, was because the Panos produced an elite—four or five men— who served (somewhat cautiously) as Lenin believed a vanguard should serve, whipping on those who were "slumbering, apathetic, bound by routine, inert and dormant" (Lenin 1975, 97–98). To that list of patronizing adjectives (applied by Lenin to the party's potential rank and file) should be added the comment that those Panos in Bisipara who did not leap to man the barricades probably held back because they saw most of the benefit going to the vanguard and not much coming to themselves.

Sindhu the schoolmaster and his younger brother, joint holders of an estate that was large by Bisipara standards, were two of the Pano leaders. Another was a former police constable, Gondho, who later stood as an independent candidate for the Orissa Assembly (and was roundly defeated) and who, when I was last in touch with Bisipara in 1959, had become secretary (appointed and salaried, not elected) of the new local government council. A fourth Pano notable, Balunki Sahani, had also been a candidate for the Assembly, competing in the Congress interest for the reserved seat in the Phulbani constituency. He too had gone down to defeat, for the area was a stronghold of the Congress party's rival, Ganatantra Parishad. At the time I knew him he was employed as a constituency agent for the Congress party, and made occasional trips on party business to the state capital, Bhubaneswar. (At that time a visit to Bhubaneswar, almost two hundred miles away, was a lifetime event for about a dozen people in Bisipara. They went to pay their respects not to politicians in the showpiece new town but to the divinity in the Lingraj temple in old Bhubaneswar.)

These men, especially the last two, who were by then virtually professional politicians, had acquired a capacity that before 1947 had been denied to Panos: they knew how to use their status as untouchables to make the government their ally in village politics. On the clean-caste side not a single person of standing had a similar level of sophistication. Nor did anyone in the clean castes have usable connections with political parties and politicians. One man, a Distiller, Basu Pradhan, had offered himself as an independent candidate and, as I recall, was so thoroughly trounced that he forfeited his deposit.[2] He later was elected chairman of the local government council, because Bisipara people thought he had the right connections with influential local officials. But it was generally believed that Basu's show of public service was mere hypocrisy and in fact a continuation of his

[2] Candidates were required to make a deposit, which was forfeited by those who did not receive at least one-sixth of the valid votes (one-twelfth in a two-member constituency). An Assembly candidate at that time deposited Rs. 250, or half that sum if the candidate was Adibasi (Scheduled Tribe) or untouchable (Scheduled Caste). Parliamentary candidates deposited twice those amounts.

main career, which was making money through commerce and taking government contracts. His influence with the sircar was in the old style, obtained by greasing palms. For sure, he was not the man to stand forward as the champion of orthodox Hinduism and the preservation of Bisipara's community in its traditional form. Another potential candidate was the respected leader of the village, the Warrior sirdar. If anyone was charged with protecting dharma it was he, and prior to 1947 he had enjoyed the open support of the administrators. But now sirdars were being written off by Orissa's new rulers as "relics of feudalism and imperialism," and some years later the office of sirdar was formally abolished. In the 1950s it was still intact, and the Bisipara sirdar at that time was, at least among his own people, an influential man.

All that weakness in the clean castes being apparent, it is not immediately obvious why, in 1953 and later, I did not see Panos entering any of the temples in the village other than the one they had built in their own street. The law of the land laid down their right of access. Their opponents, the clean castes, lacked both the political skills and the political connections to make an effective protest. The Panos, in contrast, appeared to have enough clout to make the state enforce their legitimate rights. But if they had the clout, they chose not to use it. They took care to so manage matters that their opponents in the village were not driven to violence, even though the Pano cause might conceivably have been helped by a modest riot.

In 1959 I spent a year among politicians and officials in Bhubaneswar. It was abundantly clear that Orissa, like other Indian states, had no shortage of politicians and social workers eager to hurl themselves, as latter-day Gandhis, into agitations on behalf of the oppressed. (In a few cases they had even turned agitation into a business, ferreting out extortionate merchants and raising funds by getting their protests bought off.) But nothing of that kind, legitimate or otherwise, went on in the Kondmals. The Panos, up to 1953, had received no help from professional politicians in their protests against civic disqualification, unless one counts the rather lightweight social worker, the Harijan inspector, and his preaching.

The absence of resolute and sustained outside aid would explain why the Panos did not put up a more vigorous fight, but it cannot be the whole story. When they followed the distinctly non-Gandhian way of throwing in the towel and retreating to their own street to build a Shiva temple there, they were motivated from another direction. Partly they knew there were better prizes elsewhere—at least, their leaders knew that. A larger part of the story is that all of them, the leaders and the led, were using a strategy that had for generations been habitual, alike for Panos and for clean-caste Oriyas.

Before I follow that trail, I will continue the story of what went on in Bisipara between 1953 and 1955. Events did in fact did take a turn towards violence. The Panos also made a fleeting, but significant, attempt to involve state politicians in their cause by playing the Harijan trump card.

4

Gupte Bisoi and Bali Sahani

The Edge of Violence

Prejudice against people who are different may be strong or weak because calculating individuals—ethno-politicians—work to make it so. I am sure that this often is the case, but I do not imply that all that ever happens is the intended result of someone's manipulation. None of us knows enough to control affairs in that comprehensive way; even when we do have information, we may not know how to use it effectively. For that reason—insufficient knowledge—it is difficult to predict what will happen; after the event, it is sometimes easier to explain why things turned out the way they did. The past, in principle at least, may deal with facts; the future can be encoded only as probabilities. History, in that respect, should be less hit-or-miss in its pronouncements than is social engineering, which bids to control the future.

Sometimes we are in control, at least to the extent of acting with foresight. When temple entry legislation seemed to provide the right opportunity, the Panos made a decision to confront the Warriors and the rest of the village. What they did was quite rational; they matched means to ends. Equally, if my surmise is right, when they decided to go no further with open challenges to Bisipara's orthodoxy, they were still being perfectly rational.

Frontal assaults of that kind, they may have calculated, seemed likely to cost more than they wanted to pay.

Some moves, however, in the war between the Panos and other castes in Bisipara, appear to have been quite uncalculated. People acted on the instant and without thought for the consequences. Later, other and cooler heads began to take control, working out strategies either to exploit and intensify the conflict or to put a lid on it. One such event was a chance encounter between Gupte Bisoi, a youth of Warrior caste, and Bali Sahani, a middle-aged Pano, a man of substance. I present the story as written for me by the not unprejudiced pen of Debohari Bisoi. (The calendar dates in parentheses are part of the original Oriya text and were written in roman script.)

> In the light half of [the lunar month of] Aswino on a Tuesday (October 20, 1953) Ekadosi Bisoi's son Gupte, who lives in War- rior street in Bisipara, had gone to catch fish in the Jhuliberna paddy fields. It was getting a little dark when Gupte put his fish together and started home. When Gupte was walking along a [narrow] bank between two of Jodu Bisoi's fields, Bali Sahani, who lives in Asrisai [a Pano overflow street to the north of the village], was returning from Phiringia market. He was on the same bank and they met. When they met Gupte said, "You hold on a minute. After I am clear you come on." [He used the singu- lar form for "you," which does not indicate respect.] But Bali Sahani said, "So you have gotten to be a governor, have you, and I have to clear the path for you?" [He too used the familiar form.] He gave Gupte a push and went on his way. Gupte is only a boy and the push caused him to fall into the field, and he started to wail and shout abuse. Bali Sahani replied in kind.
>
> At the time Ramo Pradhan [a Distiller] had gone to buy snuff at Pradeshi Bagho's house [Pradeshi is a Fisherman], and, hear- ing the row, he said to Pradeshi, "Pradeshi, why don't you go out and see who's making all that noise in the fields?" Pradeshi ran out and saw that Gupte was crying and came back to Ramo and said, "Let us go and sound the alarm." [This is an empty kerosene tin, hung in each street. They beat it with a stick.] Hearing the alarm, the leading men, as is the rule, came. They asked Gupte what happened, and, having heard him, they all ran after Bali to call him back. But Bali thought they were going

to murder him and ran to his own street. They could not find him, and so they sent the village watchman, Porsu Sahani, and another watchman, Narayan Sahani [Porsu's son], to summon Bali Sahani to the meeting house [in Warrior street], where they had returned. Porsu Sahani came back and said, "Bali Sahani and all the brothers in the street say that they will all come to the meeting house in the morning. That's what they said to me." Everyone in the meeting house agreed to this and went home.

Meanwhile both Harijan streets in Bisipara [Panosai and Asrisai] met, and then, in the middle of the night, they sent information to the police station in Phulbani that the Bisipara people had come with clubs and sticks to murder them. They declared that all the men in Bisipara had come with clubs and sticks and guns and made a great noise near their street, while they, in fear, had hidden themselves elsewhere.

(October 21) They laid the same information before (1) the minister of education and finance, (2) the Adibasi minister, and (3) the Harijan minister, all of whom had come to inspect the Boida ashram school. The sub-inspector of police did not come to Bisipara that day, but on October 22 he came and called everyone and questioned them individually. It was all written down and the police returned to Phulbani on October 23.

After the sub-inspector, the circle inspector arrived at seven in the morning of October 24, summoned both parties, wrote down everything, and returned to Phulbani.

After several days, on November 4 a constable arrived from Phulbani and told the Panos that their case had been dismissed. "You have seven days [to appeal]. Within that seven days decide as you will." This is what the Panos were told.[1]

The Background

The incident that began all this is easy to envisage. The setting is a path, most of it less than a foot wide and, as I recall, about fifty yards long, between two large stream-irrigated paddy fields owned by Jodu Bisoi, the village postmaster. These fields were big enough to make the drop between them three or four feet.

[1] It is a sign of the place and the times (assuming that Debohari's account is correct) that this decision was not delivered in writing and through the mail but by word of mouth.

(Had the same slope been divided into four fields, the drop between each would have been only one foot.) When people meet in such a place, unless one of them is conspicuously close to one end, the etiquette is for the junior person to give way, either by retreating or by stepping off the path into the upper field. Gupte was pushed, so he said, and fell into the lower field.

I knew Gupte, a slight youth fourteen or fifteen years old, with exhibitionist tendencies and a decided bent for mischief. He would sometimes conceal himself in a garden or behind a shed in Warrior street and let fly that very distinctive ululation that women utter when they hear of a relative's death, which brought housewives running into the street to find out who was wailing and who it was that had died. With Bali Sahani I had only the slightest acquaintance, and his face has not stayed with me. My notes show that he was a schoolmaster and that his holdings in land put him among the richest four or five Panos. I have no record of his being active either among the Pano militants or with constitutionalists like the other schoolmaster, Sindhu.

Given these profiles, if one factors out untouchability and notes the difference in age and Bali's status as a schoolmaster, and if one assumes both of them had come part way along the path, then without a doubt Gupte should have given way by stepping into the upper field. (No one wears shoes, so it is no particular hardship to step aside, even when the field is under three or four inches of water.) If it had not been dusk, they might have seen one another in time and avoided the confrontation. But it was dusk (Bisipara has a very brief twilight), and both must have been in a hurry to get home, Bali in particular, having walked seven miles each way to Phiringia market. Later, when questioned by the authorities, each claimed that he had offered to give way, as a reasonable person would, but the other did not give him a chance. It is obvious, if Debohari's brief summary of the argument is correct, that relative status was the issue, and that status was itself in a twilight, made obscure and ambiguous by the contradiction between seniority and caste. Youth owes respect to age; schoolmasters are owed respect by everyone; on the other hand, because contact pollutes, Panos should not even touch a Warrior (let alone knock him over).

Debohari's account was, I know, incorrect in some respects, being confused about the government ministers who were visiting the Boida ashram school. Boida is a Kond village twenty minutes' walk south and east of Bisipara, across the Salki river. The ashram was a government institution, a boarding school for Konds, founded in the Gandhian ideal of basic training for village life. In it Kond boys (and a few girls) learned the elements of literacy and mathematics, together with gardening and some craft skills (weaving, smithery, simple tailoring, and carpentry). They also received instruction in what the authorities deemed to be suitable performing arts (Kond dances and singing the Indian national anthem). The school was a showplace (the headmaster kept a magnificent rose garden) and a convenient stage for politicians and officials to break their journey when touring in this part of Phulbani district. Ministers and high officials were in the habit of paying visits of inspection to Gandhian institutions in remote places (thus, as one of them cynically put it to me later, racking up the mileage and travel allowances).

On this occasion the Bisipara Panos discovered that important visitors from the Orissa government had come to the Boida ashram, and they sent a deputation there to petition, as Harijans, for government protection against high-caste abuse. A government minister, it need hardly be said, is a trump card in the game of enlisting patrons.

I do not know exactly who those visitors were, but Debohari's account is surely inaccurate. Whereas the government did indeed have a minister of tribal and rural welfare (Debohari's "Adibasi minister"), a minister of education and a minister of finance (who was usually also the chief minister), the last of these certainly was not present on that occasion, and there was never a "Harijan minister." Nor, so far as I can recall, was there at that time a minister who was himself a Harijan. This minor inaccuracy, however, does not lessen the significance that Debohari and others read into the incident. On the contrary, the mistake itself suggests that Debohari could see all too clearly the weakness of his own side, for his imagination strengthened the Harijan cause with an ally who in fact did not exist.

Several other features are folded into Debohari's text, some of them not obvious. For example, he does not feel it necessary to explain that when the pursuers "could not find" the escaping Bali, this was *not* because they did not know where he was. He was in the Pano street, as they well knew, but no one of clean caste would venture there for fear of being polluted. On this particular occasion, of course, they may also have held back in a prudent anticipation of being assaulted. But even when all was sweetness and light in the village and there was no threat of violence, no clean-caste person would walk into Pano street; I have seen them make a half-mile detour to avoid doing so.[2] (The reverse rule does not apply. Panos came to clean-caste streets, but only when they had business there.) By the same token, when the clean-caste leaders sent a message for the Panos, two village watchmen, Porsu and his son Narayan, who are themselves Pano, were the messengers.

Living in the middle of his culture and its habitual frames of reference, Debohari did not think it necessary to spell out how the confrontation went instantly from the *individuals* concerned (Gupte Bisoi and Bali Sahani) to the opposed *collectivities* of clean castes (mainly the Warriors) and Pano untouchables. The phrase "all the brothers," which Debohari used when reporting the Pano delaying stratagem of promising to come to the meeting house the next morning, happens to be almost literally true, for most of the households in Pano street believed themselves to be descended from a common male ancestor. But "all the brothers" on this occasion signifies not so much descent as a potential for collective action and a perception of collective interest. Our metaphorical use of "brotherhood" (as in the International Brotherhood of Teamsters) has the same suggestion.

---

[2] Younger men of clean caste who worked for me did accompany me into Pano street. My employment, I assume, gave them ad hoc immunity.

There are stock phrases in Debohari's text (and in the many other texts that he and various other people wrote for me) that resemble Homeric repetitions, identifying standard attributes— rosy-fingered dawn, the wine-dark sea, grey-eyed Athena, the wise Telemachus. In his text, Debohari fastens not on an attribute but on a characteristic action. When government inquiries are held, "all was written down," or the inspector "wrote everything down." Those phrases carry with them a slight sense of awe, a foreboding, the idea of an immense and anonymous and un- avoidable force set in motion. My adjectives, which recall Max Weber's characterization of rational bureaucracy as an "iron cage," exactly convey the sense of unease that the sircar and its intentions aroused in the ordinary people of Bisipara. As they saw the situation, individuals, including officials and politicians, could be deceived, bribed, or flattered (increasingly, as famil- iarity with politicians bred contempt) into being a patron. But beyond those individuals was a different world marked by the act of writing, by impersonality and anonymity, the world of files and judicial inquiries, a world that was dangerous because it was inscrutable and therefore difficult to manipulate. It was a world that lay beyond the morality of the villagers, requiring, if they were not to be overwhelmed, capabilities that most of them did not have. They saw themselves living, as it were, every day un- der government as under a volcano.

Split Minds: Paranoia and Pragmatism

Apart from messages that can be read from Debohari's text, I saw other signs of a mild collective paranoia among the clean castes. In the early days of the dispute a Pano came to Jodu's post office to send a letter, and Jodu discovered, to his consterna- tion, that he had run out of two-anna stamps. He came in anx- ious haste to the bungalow to buy back some of my stock, for he feared that the Pano might complain to the government (pre- sumably to the shadowy Harijan inspector) that the Bisipara postmaster was refusing to sell stamps to Harijans. Jodu was doubly anxious since his post office had only "experimental" status.

About the same time Bala Misro, the younger brother of Oruno, the Brahmin who served Sri Ramchandro's temple (when not out of favor with the village authorities), borrowed a gun from the old Christian man who lived at one end of Warrior street. (Bala's grandmother, when widowed, married a Christian widower; she was the old man's stepmother.) Bala set off to bag green pigeons, which frequented the tall trees that fringed the village, or perhaps shoot a *gendalia*, the big black heron that feeds on small fish in the paddy fields. As he was walking north out of Warrior street he was intercepted by Debohari and his cousin Jaya, the son of the sirdar. (Jaya's great-grandfather and Debohari's grandfather were brothers. Jaya called Debohari *dadi*, which is "father's younger brother.") Jaya stopped Bala and made him turn back and told him to keep the gun out of sight or return it to his uncle. Debohari told Bala that if any of the Panos saw him walking out in the fields carrying a gun, there would surely be a report sent to the police station in Phulbani, and yet more trouble would descend on the village. Jaya was particularly sensitive, since rumor had it that the Panos had told the police that Jaya had taken his father's double-barrelled shotgun and led the assault on Pano street.

The Warrior caste group, to which Jaya and Debohari and Jodu and young Gupte all belonged, constituted the core of the clean castes. The other castes—Distillers, Potters, Herdsmen, Brahmins, and so forth—were distinct and sometimes at odds in ways that I have described, but in this particular context the clean castes held together without any problem. There was no hint of defection, no sign that anyone calculated what they might gain by going over to the other side. Evidently they all saw themselves equally threatened by the Pano refusal to accept the ritual disqualification of untouchability.

But I do not think anyone, on either side, worked out logically and systematically why that refusal should be considered a threat, and what precisely would be the consequences if the Panos gained access to the Shiva temple; everyone (of clean caste) just knew, without further question, that it would be wrong. Whatever might be the consequences, the event in itself would be intrinsically evil. Reasoning at that point seems to have come to a stop, having bottomed out on fundamental values. Panos inside Shiva's Kondmals temple would violate everyone's dharma, including their own; in our idiom, it would be something unnatural. That mind-set is the irrational base for any kind of ethnic prejudice; the matter is prejudged, not open for consideration.

That particular style of thinking—the mode of true believing that emerges when second nature is brought into consciousness—seems apparent also in something the clean castes did when the news came down that the Pano case had been dismissed and they had been given seven days to make an appeal. The clean castes sacrificed a goat to Komeswari and held a feast to eat the meat. No doubt they were celebrating what was, for the time at least, a victory; but more than simple rejoicing was involved in the gesture. Komeswari was the patron deity of the Warriors. She had a shrine built into the western end of the meeting house in Warrior street, where they stored drums and various relics of distant wars with the Konds. When they realized, from the intervention of the police, what deep trouble might be in store for them, they did what they must have done in the past when they went to war: they promised Komeswari a goat if she intervened to bring them victory. Individuals used to make the same kind of promise in times of sickness, vowing a sacrifice to this or that deity if the patient survived. Their attitude on these occasions was perfectly instrumental (which seems to us, but did not to them, a strange way to deal with a divinity): if the sick person survived, the deity got a sacrifice and they had a feast. If the patient died, nothing was done. They paid for salvation only on delivery.

The sacrifice and the sacramental feasting that followed seem to indicate a frame of mind that places the affair beyond the range where people calculate consequences and think about benefits in relation to costs. By joining in a sacrificial meal they reminded themselves that their ethnic identity, as clean castes, was in the realm of the sacred, an absolute value that could not be compromised. But when one remembers that had the authorities not dismissed the Pano case, Komeswari would not have been honored with a goat sacrifice and there would have been no sacralizing feast, the matter does not seem quite so straightforward. Payment by results surely suggests calculation, the notion, perhaps, that Komeswari's divine identity will remain in the realm of the divine only so long as there is a positive payoff from keeping it there.

Furthermore, is it not also possible that, in this case at least, ethnic identity, despite all the posturing to the contrary, was itself subject to calculations of utility? In other words, there may have been conditions in which the people of Bisipara would have asked themselves what they had to gain or lose by insisting on dharma, on the fundamental propriety of caste distinctions. What price, they might have asked, would they have to pay if they insisted to the end that untouchability was itself untouchable? Must that value be maintained, whatever the cost?

There is, by chance, evidence that suggests a clear answer to this question. The village of Boida, where the ashram school was situated, had in it a community of Panos. These were Kui Panos, that is, Panos whose first language is Kui, and they were scorned by the Oriya Panos of Bisipara. In 1955 there was a burst of trouble in Boida between the dominant caste of Konds and their Panos, culminating in one of the Panos clouting a leading Kond across the face, and doing so in the most public and most inappropriate of settings, a judicial assembly convened to resolve the dispute. The root of the problem, insofar as it was not a matter of personalities, was economic: the Boida Panos had grown too numerous to be supported in their traditional role of farm laborers. I will come to that issue later.

The solution that the Boida Konds found was partly modeled on what they knew had been done some years before in Bisipara.

They decided to punish their Panos by depriving them of the right to make music at weddings and on other festive occasions, exactly as had been done in Bisipara. But they went further and announced they would no longer hire Panos as field laborers. Boida had this falling-out in the hot weather, in April and May, when the ground is too hard for cultivation, and this may have allowed the Konds to forget that they depended on their Panos for farm labor, just as most of the Panos depended for their living on work in Kond fields. Debohari, who was Boida's schoolmaster, helped them draw up a document linking the ban on music making with a ban on employing Panos as farm laborers. While he did so, he pointed out the idiocy of the decision. But the Konds, it seemed at first, were too angry to listen to commonsense and insisted on a total ban.

It turned out to be nothing but a gesture. When the rains came in late June, individual Kond landholders and individual Pano laborers picked up where they had left off at the end of the previous harvest. Debohari, talking to me about the case and comparing it with what had been done in Bisipara, said explicitly that while people in Bisipara had a much bigger problem on their hands with their sophisticated Harijans than Boida did with its still quite jungly Kui-speaking Panos, it had never occurred to either side in Bisipara to extend the boycott into everyday economic arrangements. That would have been stupid.

I think that same pragmatic outlook underlay the clean-caste strategy in the 1950s. In response to the temple entry confrontation they presented the authorities with a front of sweet reason—at least, that is, with disingenuous suggestions about holding a referendum—instead of indulging themselves in impassioned moralistic outrage. Their practical response in the village was to inflict a token penalty on the Panos, a kind of ritual banishment, which surely irritated the Panos but did not leave them hungry and desperate. (At festivals time and again, while I lived in the village, I saw Boad Panos take over the musical instruments from their replacements. I never saw anyone object, possibly because the original Panos were much better performers.)

What Interests Were Different People Serving?

The Panos exercised their right to appeal against the dismissal of their case within the seven days. My records are confused, but so far as I can piece the story together, the appeal was lodged by November 11. The next note I have records a resolution by the village meeting (of clean castes) that everyone should hold themselves in readiness for a visit from the third officer on December 9. I know that later in December the collector (the senior administrator in Phulbani district) came to the village and held a hearing. After that I have short notes about raising a levy from each house to pay the expenses of witnesses who had to go to court in Phulbani. Eventually, on April 15, 1954, in the court of the second officer, the case came to an end. It seems that the possibility of criminal proceedings against the clean castes (for causing a riot) died with the visit of the collector to the village. Thereafter the Panos brought a civil suit, which they agreed to withdraw in the settlement of April 15. (The story has holes in it because I was away from December 1953 through much of 1954, and the events are known to me only through a diary that Debohari kept during my absence.)

I am quite sure that there was no riot "with sticks and guns" and that Debohari's account is substantially correct. They probably did chase after Bali, calling him back. If they had caught him, they might have been rough with him. Even that I doubt. Both the clean castes and the Panos were sharply aware of how unpleasant the police could be. In December and January, when the main rice harvests come in, there is usually a flurry of complaints about crop thefts perpetrated in the night. (The villagers organize a watch in the fields, a rather half-hearted affair because they know that the area is too big for them to patrol adequately.) Panos always got the blame for thefts, but everyone knew that there were some other thieves as well. This particular year (the winter of 1953–54), once the police had appeared on the scene and further inquiries were pending, there were no crop thefts reported at all.

Why then, if both parties knew that a police visitation, and certainly a longer police presence, would be unpleasant for everyone, did the Panos act so as to make official attention inescapable? They did that twice, first when they confronted the Warriors at the Shiva temple, and again several years later when they hastened through the night to lay their complaint at the Phulbani police station. I think, however, that the two occasions were fundamentally different. The temple confrontation was a deliberate strategy, thought through beforehand; otherwise they would not have given the authorities warning of their intentions. The outcome must have disappointed them: both parties got a lecture on staying out of trouble, and nothing more was done to implement the law. They then presumably made, as I have said, a reasoned decision to discontinue the tactic of local confrontations in sacred places.

Gupte's tumble in the field was obviously not part of any thought-through strategy. The encounter was an accident. The hasty complaint to the police during the night, although not accidental, certainly was impulsive. I suspect—although obviously I do not know for sure—that there was an element of panic in the Pano decision. Whether that panic was entirely spontaneous or whether it was played upon by the militants among them, again I do not know. Several crucial things were evidently done on the spur of the moment. Running seven miles along jungle and field paths at night seems to be on a level with the original encounter in the field and with the anything-but-rational sounding of the alarm when the two men found Gupte wailing and cursing at the edge of the village. The most common reason for sounding the alarm (except to summon men to the meeting house, usually a known and anticipated event) is that someone has seen a snake. The appropriate response is to seize a stick or an axe and come running. On both these occasions—Gupte's tumble and using the tocsin—people acted on impulse. I think there was an element of that also in the midnight race to bring in the police.

Once that was done, however, everything the Panos did can be construed as part of a deliberate strategy. Particularly rational (and effective) was the petition that caused the government ministers, whoever they were, to put in their word. Their involvement and the shadow of their continuing interest (even if, as is likely, the interest was quite fleeting) were enough to ensure that the local officials would rein in whatever prejudice they felt against the Panos and conduct themselves with more than usual concern for due process. For officials, by that time, the very word *Harijan* marked the location of a political minefield.

Invoking the ministers shifted the contest out of the village arena more decisively than did the earlier temple entry confrontation. The latter, of course, was set in motion by a law passed by the legislative assembly. But the message that it might have conveyed to the Warriors of Bisipara was not clearly heard, if heard at all. The lawmakers in the assembly placed themselves on the side of the Harijans; but local officials, whose job it was to enforce the law, gave Bisipara people the impression that they, the administrators, saw it all as a storm in a teacup that could be stilled by words and threats. Things were done that way under the British; indeed, that was how the villagers themselves managed their own affairs. Like village elders, the sub-inspector and his constables seemed more concerned with restoring the outward signs of order and harmony than with matters of legal principle. The Warriors must surely, on this occasion (probably 1949 or 1950), have taken away the message that the new government, the parliamentary democracy, was for practical purposes far away in Bhubaneswar, the state capital, and that its local agents had no interest in doing anything, even if mandated by the politicians, that might roil the local waters.

By the time the Gupte incident occurred, a few years later in 1953, the world had changed. Democratic principles had spread beyond Bhubaneswar, reaching even as far as Bisipara. Local officials, especially when they knew the ministers might be monitoring them, seemed almost to fall over themselves to give the Panos due process and a forum in which to assert their civic equality with the clean castes. This time the investigative process did not stop at the relatively low station of a sub-inspector of police; it went to the very summit of the local administration, the collector himself. This time the Panos did take their case to court. They did not win, it is true, but in the meantime the Warriors had been given an impressive demonstration of how to mobilize official support, a feat which they knew would have been beyond them. It had been done, moreover, by people whom the Warriors knew to be anything but favorites of the local officials. The Panos lost the case but were winning the war by demonstrating how effectively they could make even disdainful patrons work for them.

In short, the Warriors were given a dramatic, firsthand lesson in citizenship, both in the ethos of the egalitarian society, which was supposed to come into existence, and in certain new techniques of political action. I suspect they found the lesson perplexing. The Panos too, as yet unaccustomed to the ways of parliamentary democracy, must have been astonished at their own effectiveness and, through this incident, have begun to realize that the map of local political power was being redrawn. In particular the influence that leading politicians had over local officials, and what it could mean to have the backing of those politicians, must have been made abundantly clear.

The authorities—police and revenue officials alike—I am sure were well aware that the main charge was a fabrication and that no one from the clean castes had gone marauding in the night, armed with a gun. (There were only four guns in the village, and none of their owners would for a second have risked the confiscation of such a prized possession.)[3] In normal circumstances the first visit from the sub-inspector, together with the veiled threats that are uttered by the police on such occasions, would have ended the affair. But normality was skewed by the accidental presence of political dignitaries and by the nearness of the ashram school. The circle inspector, at least in 1953, was a mighty person; in the eyes of the villagers the collector was on a level with the Almighty.

[3] I refer to breach-loading shotguns, one of them double-barreled. There were also two or three muzzle-loaders, valued possessions certainly, but known to be tricky to load and, if not discharged, perilous to unload.

Six years after independence the collector and his subordinates in the revenue hierarchy (in this case the second and the third officers) were no doubt well aware that only a foolish official would treat requests from a politician lightly. They knew that questions asked in the Assembly (during question time, when members held the ministers and their officials to account), particularly questions about the mistreatment of Harijans, might later block promotion or cause a transfer to some posting even more undesirable than Phulbani. The officials therefore took pains to see that the judicial rights of the Panos were scrupulously and conspicuously respected, although most officials had no high opinion of Panos and probably would have been glad to let the police handle the matter in their usual brusque way. The Warriors of Bisipara, especially those who, like Debohari, were relatively well informed about public affairs, were surely demoralized when it came home to them that their own Bisipara Panos had managed to cause this unprecedented display of judicial exertion. The Panos themselves, as I said, were probably not only awed but (some of them) made uneasy by their own success in manipulating the raj (villagers like to use that name for government when it does something for them). There were risks in too blatant a triumph; clean-caste employers gave many of them work, and the raj mostly did not.

Neither these events in the secular world of litigation nor the underlying prudence displayed by both sides dissuaded the Warriors and the clean castes from continuing to frame their strategies in the mode of true belief, at least to themselves. But even this framing did not conceal an element of pragmatism. Here is Debohari's account of what they did.

On November 13, 1953, in the Bisipara meeting house at about ten in the morning the leading men of the village held a meeting in order to be strong in unity. The reason for the meeting was this. Panosai had appealed to the police station over the Gupte trouble. When this was dismissed they brought a case against us in the courts. Therefore we all held a meeting to ensure our unity.

In the morning all the village people [adult males of clean

caste] bathed and assembled near Sri Ramchandro's temple, bringing what offerings they could find. When all were assembled they went to the temple and the Brahmin Ganesa lit incense sticks and made puja. We all shouted "Haribolo!" [called on God] and said we were all of one voice. Then we shared in the offerings and went home, having arranged that we should meet in the evening and write that we were united.

We assembled in the evening. The bell was sounded [the kerosene tin] and everyone came to the meeting house. The meeting began. A document was written saying whoever revealed our doings to the Panos should pay a fine of twenty-five rupees and the money should be deposited with the village authorities.

The anticipatory threat of a fine on those who do not keep their promise is standard in such documents; it is an attempt to impart to the decision the instant majesty of the written word. The amount always is twenty-five rupees. The sacrament at Sri Ramchandro's temple was evidently considered not enough in this case and they provided this secular penalty as a fail-safe device. I cannot make much sense of the phrase "reveal our doings to the Panos," for all they did in the meeting was threaten potential backsliders and impose levies on themselves to pay the expenses of the witnesses who might have to go to court. I suppose the oath was intended to be a morale booster, but, as with almost everything else in Bisipara that touched the divinity, this occasion too had its revenue-enhancing features. I have a further note that much later, a week or so before the final decision was reached in the Phulbani courts before the second officer, they held a meeting in Market street in front of the houses of two people who had persistently avoided paying their levies, to shame them. Collecting money, not only moral solidarity, was an issue in that meeting, as in many others.

Facade and Reality

It is clear to me now that the conflict that I have so far described, between the clean castes and the Panos of Bisipara, can reasonably be considered racial or ethnic, without unduly stretching either of those terms. At the time (the 1950s) it seemed to be enough to use the word *caste* and thus confine the significance of what was going on to the Indian scene. But the case has a wider application. Both concepts—race and ethnicity—are used in many cultures as unquestionable criteria for the distribution of moral status. Biological (racial) or ethnic (customary) distinctiveness separate the worthy from the unworthy. *Ethnic*, suggesting culture, happens to be the favored term at present, still having a quasi-scientific, quasi-objective respectability that *racial*, arguing politics from biology, has lost. Cultural diversity, as a concept, is politically correct at this time; genetic diversity, especially when it concerns the distribution of talent, is not. But in practice, folk prejudices—in Bisipara and elsewhere in the world—seem to combine both notions: the Other is inevitably disgusting with respect to dietary habits or sexual appetites or whatever else, and this is because the Other was born that way. The difference is part of an unchangeable natural order, therefore compromise is out of the question, because the Others could not change their ways even if they wanted to.

A cast of mind that is deeply impassioned (and therefore essentially mindless) is prone to release "inner energies which can be satisfied only through fight"; then conflict becomes "its own purpose and content" (Simmel 1964, 28). At that point the contestants, one would expect, will launch themselves irrevocably towards the extremes of violence, as they are doing now in the former Yugoslavia and some other parts of the world. But in Bisipara that did not happen. No heads were broken, no property was destroyed, and actual physical violence was nothing but Gupte's tumble into a paddy field. Evidently, as I have several times said, both sides, Panos and the clean castes, had calculated the cost of resorting to violence, both short-run costs in the form of police intervention and the long-run costs of damage to the politically advantageous image of a law-abiding citizen firmly committed to Gandhian nonviolence.

But this commitment, it should by now be clear, was anything but the result of a genuine Gandhian morality. Neither within

Bisipara nor in the discourse with officials was there much talk of brotherhood, of cooperation, of equality, of a common humanity that made everyone equal through their particular contributions to the common weal. Only the Harijan inspector talked that way, when he came to lecture people in Bisipara. "We are one brotherhood. They [Panos] found nothing to eat and so they ate things that are forbidden. In truth they are poor people. That is why they are untouchable. Do not we, ourselves, when a cow dies, give them the carcass knowing they will eat it?" Debohari wrote down those words, but they did not stick in the villagers' memory. What they remembered was the threat to fine them five hundred rupees if they so much as used the word "untouchable."

There was no real violence in Bisipara at that time, but the threat of violence underlay all the moves, including the compromises and concessions that each side made. Negotiation everywhere is mostly an exchange of threats, and negotiating skill is the art of knowing when to take threats seriously (or make threats that seem serious) and how to read or insert hidden offers of compromise in threats. Warriors armed with battle-axes around the Sibhomundiro were actors on stage, playing their part in a performance initiated by other actors, the Panos, each side hoping to gain favorable notice from the police and the authorities. The leisurely arrival of the three-man riot squad shows clearly that the sub-inspector and his two men did not expect to reach Bisipara and find severed heads and mutilated corpses lying around the temple. The authorities also knew how to distinguish cultural performances from reality. But, playacting though it was, violence was certainly a central and compelling theme in the drama. The threat of it moved the authorities to action.

When the Panos sent their midnight report to the police station, the minor act of violence that had in fact occurred went unmentioned, and in its place was a tale calculated to catch official attention. Such tales have traditionally been the nightmare of local officials in India—civil disorders that require forceful suppression. A collector who could not by bluff and diplomacy avert communal violence, and who had to call in the military, was in British days the archetypical tragic figure in the drama of professional failure. In Bisipara, everyone concerned who knew the place, villagers and officials alike, knew that there had been no significant violence and there would be none. But, at the same time, all were willing to frame the whole affair in the idiom of an underlying surge of riotousness. In India, of course, that is by no means an evident fantasy: actual violence between castes and religious communities, as everyone knew then and still knows, sometimes grossly disfigures civil society.

A mind set to define every situation in terms of potential violence (even when this is known to be pretence) has difficulty in taking seriously Gandhian discourses about universal brotherhood, the notion that, as John Donne put it, "any man's death diminishes me, because I am involved in mankinde." So far as Warriors were concerned, no Pano was a part of "mankinde," and the Panos felt the same about the Warriors. Logically, the theme of a common humanity must be excluded from their discourse because it would contradict the basic claim, the axiom, that the others were, by the authority of nature itself (that is, in another idiom, by God's command), disqualified from the privilege of moral *equality* (while still qualifying for a place in Bisipara's moral community).

Throughout the period when I knew Bisipara, however, this unquestioned conviction was never allowed to so direct calculations that conflict became "its own purpose and content." So far, my explanation for such prudent restraint has been only that people were afraid of the police or of losing their jobs or of having no workers to farm their land. I now want to explore more closely the context—the experiences—that went along with that pragmatic outlook on the world.

Making a Living

Marginal People

My dialect of English had in it a verb that I do not hear now, and that surely would be considered an ethnic slur: to *gyp*, which meant to cheat or swindle. The *Concise Oxford Dictionary* derives it (hesitantly) from the word used in Cambridge University for a college servant (a "gyp"), which descends from an old term for a scullion, which in turn came from an obsolete French word for a man's short tunic. Alternatively, the origin is a Greek word signifying a vulture, because the gyp "runs away with everything he can lay his hands on." Our folk etymology was less ingenious: gypping was what Gypsies did. Gypsies swindled and stole (they even stole children). They knew how to put the evil eye on you, they told fortunes, they had supernatural powers. They also lived outside the law, they traveled about, had "no fixed abode" (a sure sign of criminal tendencies), and they were smart in the ways of the world, especially smart (and untrustworthy) as horse-copers. They were not like the rest of us: they had a language of their own, they were another kind of people, they were a different race. There was an instant comprehension among ordinary working people (this was Britain in the 1930s and in wartime) of why Hitler should lump together Jews and Gypsies, even when they thought his program for dealing with that "problem" another good reason for being at war with him.

Two or three times while I lived in Bisipara, Gypsies came visiting. The local name for them was "Banjara."[1] When they came, doors were closed and anything moveable put in a safe place, even in Panosai. I had already noticed our servant do exactly that with our children's small toys when there were Pano children near the bungalow. But the connection between Pano and Banjara is one that I alone made. No one in Bisipara suggested racial or cultural affinities between them. Obviously not; there could be no racial connection because Panos and Banjara did not intermarry. Nor were the Panos rootless travelers; they had an abode. They were, as I described earlier, an integral part of Bisipara's social framework. But I could see some common features. Panos were not travelers, but in the course of making a part of their living they did travel around and, in a slightly different sense, they were believed to be relatively "traveled": particularly in Kond villages, they had experience of a wider world that was denied to others more centrally integrated into the community's social framework. In that sense they were deviant, on the margins, near the limits. They were not ordinary people.

To be out of the ordinary is not the same as being racially or ethnically distinct, even when extraordinary talents are explained as genetic gifts. A talent for music or painting or writing or financial skulduggery or dancing or banditry or playing baseball only becomes racial when it also marks a group that is already racially distinct (a matter of breeding) and/or culturally distinct (a matter of custom). Nevertheless, distinctive ways of life or distinctive occupations requiring distinctive talents do reinforce perceptions of ethnic difference. Indeed, in the absence of such obvious physical indicators as skin color, ethnic difference can only be marked by inventing or exaggerating cultural differences.

---

[1] A related Ango-Indian term, *brinjarry*, signifies a traveling merchant or dealer in grain. The people who visited Bisipara were not so grand.

In India, given the caste system, the distinction of breeding is readily available as an index of difference. Caste, moreover, also picks out occupation for the same purpose (in a somewhat unsystematic way), as when scavenging and music making index a Pano. But the Panos were also marked in other ways. Like the Gypsies they were assumed to be deviants, lawbreakers. Like the Gypsies, they were not landowners but traders and entrepreneurs, who created markets used by stay-at-home, unsophisticated, honest, simple-minded, hard-working people. To describe the common Kondmals perception of a Pano those adjectives need only be inverted: Panos were without roots, cunning, dishonest, smart, and living on their wits. The same opprobrium serves to mark a Gypsy, or a Jew (outside Israel), or an Indian in East Africa, or a Levantine in West Africa. The negative attributions then may become materials to justify or sometimes to camouflage ethnic prejudice. Hostility that in reality is mindless and irrational is rationalized on the ground that the despised people are despised not only for what they are but also for the harm they do. In particular, they are to blame for the economic hardships or the setbacks that ordinary people suffer. Behind this camouflage of reasoning lurks the notion of intrinsic, unquestionable, primordial evil. (If others did not do what they do, they would not be despised. But they could not do otherwise because nature made them that way. The implied offer of inclusion is withdrawn, even as it is made.)

Those primordial judgments did not much occur in Kondmals discourse. Panos were regarded by ordinary people as cheats and lawbreakers, but negative judgments about them in that respect remained well below the threshold of impassioned racism. It seems, as I suggested earlier, almost as if ethnicity was so prominent and so ubiquitous in the culture—everyone belonged to a minority—that it was taken for granted even to the point of sometimes going unnoticed. If hostility towards any group was to be justified, it had to be done on the grounds of what people did, not what they were. What they were, after all, was a matter of dharma, and no one could be blamed for following that (even

A Kui Pano, Naika. He had been taken in as a child-servant by a Sweeper family in Bisipara.

Kartiko Kohoro, one of the few Konds who lived in Bisipara. The sirdar annoyed Distillers by allotting him a garden in their street.

if what they had done in earlier lives—their karma—had got them where they were now).

Panos as Middlemen

I cited earlier a passage written by Macpherson about the Panos:

> The Panwa is proverbially indispensable to every Khond hamlet. His duties are to provide human victims . . . ; to carry messages, such as summonses to council or to the field; to act as a musician at ceremonies, and to supply the village with cloth. . . . They use both the Khond and the Oriyah languages. . . . They are treated with great kindness, but as an inferior and protected, perhaps a servile race. They are never neglected at a feast; and any injury done to them is promptly resented. But they are never allowed to bear themselves as equals. (1865, 65)

Macpherson's enemy, Campbell, had this to say:

> Each [Kond] village has its own chief, or Mulleko, and with him is joined an officer, called Digaloo, or interpreter, of the Panoo caste, a race most useful to the Khond tribes, although they regard them as greatly their inferiors. . . . they transact all business for the Khonds, who consider it beneath their dignity to barter or traffic, and who regard as base and plebeian all those who are not either warriors or tillers of the soil. . . . These Panoos are base and sordid miscreants, who, without the excuse of superstition or ignorance, carry on a profitable trade in the blood of their fellow-men. . . . Their guilt admits of no palliation, and no mercy is ever shown them when they are brought up for punishment. (1864, 50–53)

Campbell's reasoning is less clear than his prejudices. Why should Panos too not be given "the excuse of superstition or ignorance" when they are to be punished, presumably for kidnapping meriah victims? Evidently profit-takers are, in Campbell's definition, neither superstitious nor ignorant and therefore must be cynical about their religion and cannot use it to palliate their guilt.

These two Scotsmen were not alone in their admiration for the Konds. In various published documents that I have seen, including *Taylor's Manual*, an interleaved foolscap-size gazetteer kept in the Kondmals subdivisional office, printed about the end of the century and extensively annotated by a succession of subdivisional officers, and in a manuscript on the Konds written by an official who served there in the 1930s[2]—in all of these there is a transparent ethnic prejudice in favor of the Konds: Konds, unlike Panos, were honest. The same notion was part of local folklore. From Bisipara Oriyas and from Konds themselves I several times heard it said that (until recently) one could leave a bag of gold coins in a Kond street, and come back a month later, and find that no one had stolen even a single coin. (I wonder who among them had ever seen a bag of gold coins, or even a single gold coin.)

Macpherson liked almost everything about Konds. "The Khonds are fitted by physical constitution to undergo the severest exertions and to enjoy every form of privation. Their forms are characterized by strength and symmetry. The muscles of the limbs and body are clean and boldly developed." This wholesomeness is linked with how they make a living. "The pursuit of agriculture, varied by war and the chase, is exclusively held in honour. There are no renters of land or labourers for hire." Here is his summary: "The distinguishing qualities of the character of the Khonds appear to be these: a passionate love of liberty, devotion to chiefs, and unconquerable resolution. They are besides faithful to friends, brave, hospitable, and laborious" (1865, 60, 62, 81).

In Macpherson's mind, in Campbell's mind, and in the minds of the Konds themselves these noble qualities go along with a

---

[2] H. W. Alderson's *The Khonds and the Khondmals*, which I saw in London, was never, so far as I know, published. In India I saw a very similar manuscript, with the same title, written by a man who had been Alderson's head clerk. That manuscript too, I believe, did not find a publisher.

refusal to engage in commerce. Konds grew turmeric. They always marketed it through middlemen, mainly from Oriya villages like Bisipara. No true Kond ever set himself up as a trader or even tried to cut out the small middlemen by taking his crop directly to a merchant-shopkeeper. When I suggested they could do so, I got two kinds of reply. One, entirely rational, was that the merchant-shopkeepers would not credit a Kond with the middleman's commission because they needed to keep intact their network of small traders. The other answer was not rational—at least not as economists see rationality. A Kond who traded demeaned himself and would lose the respect of his fellow Konds because a good Kond did not trade; trade was not in their nature. (One Kond, living in Bisipara—the man who wanted to build a house in Distiller street—did trade in turmeric and, as a result, occasionally came in for abuse from other Konds.)

Nineteenth- and early twentieth-century administrators of the British Empire—those who might have styled themselves the bearers of Kipling's "white man's burden"—are well known for what is appropriately called a dumb admiration for those of their subjects (and others not their subjects) whom they believed to be martial, manly, and given to violence. They adored the Bedouin. The Masai—tall, brutal, brave, and grossly uncivilized—were yet considered splendid people. There were songs about the Zulu warrior. India had its contingent of so-called "martial" races: the Rajputs, the Jats, the Sikhs, the various warlike tribes of the northwest frontier, and above all the Gurkhas of Nepal. These were all accorded respect because, I suppose, they exemplified the values of the British upper classes and their public schools. (Despite their name, these schools were private, expensive, and the more or less exclusive domain of the upper classes.) These values included, first, physical hardiness; second, a curious combination of individual self-respect and of unswerving, mindless, almost racial devotion to the herd—that is, to people like themselves—and an equally unswerving contempt for those on the outside; and, third and not least, a marked disdain for *clever* people. Brains took second place to character. You could rely on people like the Konds: nothing "base and plebeian" about them. They were men of honor, men of their word, men of the sword. You could not feel the same way about people engaged in trade and commerce, people who were glib and clever but at the same time mere go-betweens (a wonderful irony when one remembers that both Macpherson and Campbell, although not themselves traders, were employees of the East India Company).

In the Kondmals one contrast with the noble, straightforward primitive Kond was provided by the devious, commerce-minded, bilingual Pano, who, unlike the Konds of those days, spoke both Kui and Oriya—the "Digaloo," Campbell's "base and sordid miscreant."

Panos were "miscreants" and shown "no mercy" because the object of their commerce—at least the object that Campbell and Macpherson noticed—was the meriah, the person destined to be a victim of human sacrifice. Mixed in with this sentiment, I have suggested, was a general idea that commerce is of itself a soiling activity. Konds, obviously, attached no moral stigma to the provision of meriah victims, but they did consider trade to be work for inferior people. How and why such feelings come into being, I do not know; perhaps it is because the farmers are also the warriors, and it is the mark of warriors everywhere to despise those who do not bear arms. But I do know that the sentiment seems always to lead to resentment, a curiously paradoxical situation in which those who scorn trade and traders nevertheless know that traders have power. If, on top of that, the traders are racially or ethnically distinct, economic resentment shifts easily into the deeper mindlessness of ethnic or racial prejudice. That has been the fate of Jews in Europe, of Gujeratis in East Africa, and of Lebanese and Syrians in West Africa.

In the 1950s Panos in the Kondmals were still part-time traders. Bisipara Panos, like other Oriyas, dealt in turmeric, as did a few Panos from Kond villages (none from Boida, so far as I knew). Panos also dealt in hides and leather (a monopoly of untouchable castes), and they traded in cattle markets, including some down on the plains to the south of the Kond hills. They (some of them) were still in the 1950s regarded as well traveled, smart, quick to seize the advantage, and thoroughly untrustworthy. They were also the objects of ethnic prejudice.

But their trading and commerce did not alone put them in that special position, not at least in Bisipara. One reason was that Panos were not the only practitioners of the art of the fast deal. They shared the field with the rest of the Oriya speakers, of all castes, even Brahmins. Nor were they the champions. When it came to commercial exploitation, no episode even approached the monstrous out-still system that so much enriched the Distillers. Although numerous, Panos were relatively small players in the game.

It follows, second, that whatever victims the Bisipara Pano traders found, these were mostly *not* other Oriyas in Bisipara. Accusations of exploitation and cheating, gypsy style, only played a minor role, if any, in Bisipara's near miss with ethnic violence. On the contrary, the Panos themselves could, and did, claim to have been economically exploited. But the wider communicative skills that lie behind trade and commerce (recall Campbell's translation of the Pano lineage name of Digaloo as "interpreter") have a different significance. As will become clear, Bisipara's Panos in the 1950s were putting their entrepreneurial and communicative skills to a different use: to gain political power.

In short, Bisipara's Panos were not like Jews or Gypsies; commercial skills did not intensify ethnic difference and ethnic prejudice. Economic matters, however, may have been relevant in several other ways. Material deprivation and its consequences can intensify ethnic hatreds. The type case occurs in the inner cities of the present-day United States. Deprivation leads to violence and lawlessness, which are then attributed to the ethnicity of the offenders. That, too, was the message in Sindhu's text, when he wrote about Ollenbach as the Panos' savior.

The Boida Outlaws

I had a long talk with a Kond from Boida, Lonkera Kohoro, about the brouhaha with the Panos that had gone on in his village. Lonkera was in the middle of it, being one of the two Konds clouted by a Pano (the assailant's name was Buda Digalo). It was Lonkera who, more than anyone else, forced through the decision to boycott Pano farm laborers (not just the musicians, as they had done in the more prudent Bisipara). The resolution read in part:

> From now on no one will give fire or tobacco to the Panos. They will not be called to funerals or feasts. If anyone has made a loan to a Pano, then he will press to have it back. If anyone has given them a *mahua* tree, then he will take it back.[3] In the same way those who have lent gardens to Panos, as their vassals, must take them back. Anyone who breaks these rules must pay a fine of twenty-five rupees to the panchayat.

Lonkera was an articulate man, a rival of his distant "brother," Podo Kohoro, who was the village headman. Lonkera never passed up an opportunity to seize the initiative when the more slow-spoken and slow-witted Podo let it slip. On this occasion Podo happened to have been elsewhere, and on his return he was happy to blame everything on Lonkera's short temper and his incapacity for handling Panos the right way. Podo, he himself indicated, was trusted by "his" Panos and they would not have given him any trouble. He'd have given them a good telling-off, he told me, and they would have said they were sorry and that would have been the end of it. He exuded the kind of effortless superiority that mixes with noblesse oblige to create a colonial patriarch or an army officer (that was the model for the army I knew). No one in Bisipara talked that way about their Panos, although the sirdar did have at least the outward form of a paternal relationship with some Panos, in particular those appointed as Bisipara's watchmen. The pattern for such interaction is, of course, the feudal relationship between a lord and his vassal.

Podo, when he talked that way, was recalling a past that no

---

[3] This refers to the privilege of collecting the tree's flowers to make liquor or its nuts to press oil. The tree is *Bassia latifolia* or *Madhuca latifolia*. A single tree, it is said, can produce more than fifty kilograms of flowers in a season.

longer existed, at least not in the simple paternalistic entirety that he supposed. He might indeed have managed to calm the angry Panos. They did defer to him, but not much in the idiom of feudalism. More likely, I suspect, they were deferential because he was a large man with a formidable temper and a tendency, especially with a drink or two in him, to become violent. He was also, by Boida's standards, a wealthy landowner, and some of the Boida Panos depended on him for their living.

Lonkera had a different image of his village community, more up-to-date and framed somewhat in the model of political economy. Boida Konds were the employers and Boida Panos were their workers. A survey I made there showed that this indeed was the case. Boida Panos had title to a few fields, but there were no substantial landowners among them on a level with Sindhu and his peers in Bisipara. Nor were any of the Boida Panos educated; none had government jobs. They maintained themselves partly as weavers contracted to a government-run cooperative in Phulbani (more than half the Pano houses in Boida had a loom), but mainly as farm laborers engaged by the day or sometimes for the season by Kond landowners. Occasionally at the beginning of the hot season after most of the crops were harvested, Boida Panos found temporary laboring work as road menders for the Public Works Department.

The problem, Lonkera said, was simple to diagnose but not easy to fix. There were too many Panos. Of course the example of the Bisipara Sahanis and the whole Harijan business did not help: "We brought the Panos and set them up here. Since the government has started calling them Harijans, they no longer obey us. If anyone says anything to them, they come out for a fight." But, Lonkera said, it was not simply a matter of Panos inflating their own importance. The reality was a large number of strapping young Pano men who had not enough work and plenty of time and energy to swagger around making trouble. Lonkera's own humiliation came out of just those circumstances. One of the Kond brotherhood had brought a bride for his son, and a wedding feast was being held. It was the custom to in-

Lonkera Kohoro, a Kond. He faces eastward toward the valley in which
the Boida hamlets lay. The main road to Phulbani runs across the middle
ground. Just beyond it, and below the tiered paddy fields, is a large tank
built by Dinarosingh Kohoro in the hope that this good work would
cause a son to be born to him.

Debohari and Lonkera, mapping paddy fields in Boida.

clude in the feast the Pano musicians who had come from the
bride's village to escort the wedding party. Boida's own musicians were also to be feasted. But on this occasion not just the
musicians but "half the street," as Lonkera put it, sat down and
expected to be fed. He gave the freeloaders a tongue-lashing and
sent them away. That night the Boida Panos slashed the skins of
the visitors' drums. (I never found out why their anger was
vented in that direction. Perhaps the visiting Panos had not
shown enough solidarity. Perhaps it was just a drunken esca-
pade.) Later, when the wedding celebrations were over, Lonkera
called a meeting, summoning the Panos to answer for their conduct. That was the occasion on which he and another Kond were
slapped by Buda Digalo. There would have been real violence,
Lonkera said menacingly (and to save face), if the Panos had not
promptly fled to the safety of their own street. A day later the
Konds held a meeting and instituted the total boycott (which
never was implemented).

There were no bleeding-heart overtones in the way Lonkera
talked about demographics and underemployment. There were,
as he saw it, too many Pano youths hanging around with nothing to do but make mischief, and there were enough of them to
be a physical threat. A more detached observer might have reasoned that underemployment caused deprivation and deprivation led to disorderly conduct. But whether the people or the
system got the blame, the hard fact was that the Pano population
in Boida had grown beyond the point where Panos could all be
supported exclusively as the humble dependents of their Kond
masters.

They did, however, have other ways to make a living. By the
meager standards of the Kond hills, the Panos did not go hungry—at least no more than many other people. So the cause of
the unrest, such as it was, could not have been material deprivation alone. Could, then, their intransigence have arisen from the
indignities put upon them as untouchables, from being shamed?
That was precisely what the Panos themselves identified as the
cause of the present trouble: "You invited us to the feast and so

we came. Then, in front of the visitors, why did you make a show of us and abuse us and drive us away?" In this there is a shadowy resemblance to the situation of the Bisipara Distillers: perhaps Boida Panos considered they were no longer so dependent economically that they had to put up with the humiliations that traditional dependency entailed.

The same indeterminacy between material needs and defiant self-respect as the cause of resistance can be read into tales that Lonkera, Podo, Debohari, and the Bisipara sirdar (rarely so communicative) told me about a series of episodes that took place sometime in the first twenty years of this century. (I date it at that time because a hero in the tale—as told by the Bisipara sirdar—was the wily Ollenbach, who served as the subdivisional officer of the Kondmals between 1901 and 1924.) The tale is about Kusnia and Rungo Digalo. They were two Pano brothers who lived in Kendriguda, a hamlet that is part of the cluster that makes up Boida village. (Legendary heroes and legendary villains, including recent ones like Kusnia and Rungo, whose escapades are recorded also in the official records, seem often to come in pairs in the Kond hills.) They were not, Lonkera said, the ancestors of the present Digalos who were making trouble; the latter had been brought to Boida in his grandfather's time. The descendents of Kusnia and Rungo now lived in Phulbani. They had been forcibly removed from Boida by the administration and settled in Phulbani, close to the police barracks, where they could be kept under surveillance.

Kusnia and Rungo were notorious thieves. They used to steal goats and cows and oxen and water buffaloes and sell them or eat them. (The water buffalo is a draught animal, still in the 1950s used by the Konds for sacrifice in place of the human meriah.) No one who owned a field in the vicinity of Kendriguda was getting his full harvest of paddy because Kusnia and Rungo and their gang raided the fields at night, just as the harvest was ripening. (For "gang" Lonkera used the Oriya word *dolo*, which also is a faction or political party.) Eventually the law caught up with them and Ollenbach put the two brothers in jail along with

The meriah rite in a Kond village. When human sacrifice was forbidden, the Konds first substituted monkeys, which officials soon decided too much resembled people. The victim now (1950s) is a buffalo.

other men from their gang. Sometime later they broke out and fled, separating into two outlaw bands, one going north and establishing a hideout near Katrangia, and the other, which included the two brothers, going south to Kadapodera on the Ganjam side. From these strongholds they raided the neighboring countryside.

Those who told me the tale of the two Pano outlaws were either Konds (Lonkera and Podo) or Oriyas of the Warrior caste (Debohari and the sirdar). No doubt they told it as they saw it; for them the Panos were audacious and unmitigated villains. Besides, I soon realized, the two Warriors were pleased to tell me semi-heroic tales about the "sahibs" (the white administrators) of the past, about Ollenbach in particular, how clever he was, how stern he was, how just he was, how well he could speak the Kui language, and how he joined in Kond dances. I can imagine the story of Kusnia and Rungo being told in a different way, not so much by Panos (Sindhu and one or two of his friends were the only Panos with whom I had regular conversations, and they despised the uneducated Kui-speaking Panos of Boida), but by imaginative historians who would have seen in Kusnia's and Rungo's exploits the seeds of a revolution against colonial oppression, a small window opening between false consciousness and political reality. At the very least they might have diagnosed social banditry, a proto-revolutionary phenomenon in which the victims are the rich and powerful and what is stolen goes to help the poor and the oppressed. But no one talked of Kusnia and Rungo in such a way as to suggest that they saw them as we see Robin Hood.

Social banditry commends itself to writers with a goitred social conscience because it seems to provide evidence of system malfunction, of popular unrest, of oppression, of gentry and clerics exploiting a hapless peasantry. Since social bandits are by definition on the side of the oppressed, robbing the rich and giving to the poor, then (the reasoning is) they must have received both moral and practical support from the suffering masses. Poor people shelter them from the authorities, and they emerge in academic folklore as emanations of popular discontent. Although there is little evidence that the bandits in question ever gave anything to the poor or even refrained from robbing them, the assumption nonetheless is that if they managed to stay in business as outlaws even a short time, then they must have been sheltered by the poor; therefore they must have been *social* bandits and not ordinary criminals.

That reasoning has holes in it. It may be true that ordinary people do not (always) betray outlaws and that they do (sometimes) give them shelter, but this is only because outlaws intimidate them. Even when they are in sympathy with the bandits and hate the authorities, ordinary people may be less than enthusiastic about resistance. I have not lived close to social banditry, but stories that I heard of the partisan fighting against the Germans and the Fascist authorities in 1943 and 1944 in northern Italy made me realize that such situations are rarely clear-cut. Ordinary citizens in those mountain villages for the most part gave tacit support to the partisans (who were often their sons and brothers) and rarely betrayed them. But they sometimes saw them less in the long perspective of history, as liberators and patriots, than as a source of immediate grief. The Fascist authorities punished partisan activity by punishing villagers. The partisans were safely away in the mountains and the villagers were still within reach.

Kusnia and Rungo survived for several years as outlaws. As I have suggested, they did not survive because they were social bandits enjoying the protection of ordinary people, and they were surely not politically conscious resisters against an oppressive regime. What kept them out of Ollenbach's jail was Kond hills demography and a thin administration. There were a lot of empty places in the Kond hills;[4] and in those days the fastest way of transmitting information (in the Kondmals) was a man running. The people were mostly illiterate; there were no "wanted" posters, no telephones, no radios. Many people who encountered Kusnia and Rungo would not have known they were outlaws, and those who did know probably did not see it as any of their business so long as Kusnia and Rungo did them no harm. That this is not a fanciful description of the state of communications in the Kond hills at that time is suggested by three stories told about how Ollenbach eventually got the better of the outlaws.

No one knew where the Katrangia gang lived until one day a Kond, searching for a buffalo that had strayed deep into the forest, climbed a hill and there, in a clearing, found a hamlet of Panos, with houses and gardens, and not only the gang members but also women and children. He came home and talked to people about it and eventually the news reached Ollenbach, who mustered a posse of the few police at his disposal, together with a militia of men like the Bisipara sirdar's father and the village watchmen. They surrounded the hill where the settlement lay and moved in by night. In the darkness many of the outlaws escaped. One of those who did not was captured by the sirdar's own father, who, by his son's account, did sterling work that night.

---

[4] The 1901 census indicates a population of about eighty per square mile.

The gang near Kadapodera, which was led by Kusnia and Rungo, did not take much trouble to stay out of sight. Kui-speaking Panos, like the Konds, have an institution that they call *dangari idu*, the maidens' house. This is a dormitory in which girls and boys meet to sing, tell stories, sometimes dance, and eventually pair off and sleep together. Maidens' houses were still to be found in the 1950s. Since almost all the families in a Kond village consider themselves descended from one ancestor, the girls and boys born there think of each other as brother and sister and cannot marry; nor are they supposed to bed one another. A girl marries out and goes to live in her husband's village. In courting, this procedure reverses itself; parties of boys, or sometimes individuals, can be seen in the late evening heading away from home to spend the night with the girls of another village. Good manners require a discreet arrival, after dusk, and an equally unobtrusive departure in the morning. Good manners also require older people to keep a rein on their natural curiosity about adolescent courtship, even about asking who the visitors are. There was, however, nothing shady or furtive about the institution itself; the young people have themselves a party and everyone knows it. (Married men were supposed to stay home, but it was not unknown for young Kond wives to complain about straying husbands: "I did not come here just to be fed. Rice I could get in my father's house . . .")

The Panos of Kadapodera had a maidens' house and from time to time it was visited by Kusnia and Rungo and their gang. Ollenbach, no doubt through his network of headmen and watchmen, heard of this and quietly arranged that one night there would be a large amount of liquor on hand for the young partygoers. The stratagem worked, but not perfectly. Ollenbach and his men walked into the place early the next morning and captured some of the outlaws, still fuddled with drink. Kusnia escaped "through the thatch" (a tantalizing detail that makes me regret I did not ask for more). Rungo escaped as well, and the two leaders and the remainder of their followers fled the area. They went northwards and found themselves a new base in the forest near a village called Poknaga, which lies only three miles north of Boida. The place is also hardly three miles from Bisipara.

I do not know how long they stayed there. By that time, I would guess, the administration had moved its headquarters to Phulbani, which also is near Poknaga—about four miles north. Perhaps Rungo and Kusnia kept quiet, so that even if Ollenbach's network of agents knew roughly where they could be located, no one thought it worthwhile getting an expedition together. Whatever the reason, the outlaws felt secure enough to join again in the festivities of neighboring villages.

One of these villages was Gonjagura, a mile across the river from Bisipara and a mile north of Boida. Gonjagura, an Oriya village, was holding a *tolo jatra*, a drumming festival. The musicians from invited villages come to perform through the day and into the night. These are well-attended affairs, and people who like to drink find the drumming festival a good occasion to do so. Kusnia and Rungo and their gang attended; so did Panos from Boida and many Konds. Among them was Boida's most influential man, Dinarosingh, a noted confidant of Ollenbach. (He was that same Dinarosingh who used the connection to cheat several of his Kond brothers out of their land—not a much loved man. The Boida ashram school was built on land donated to the government by one of his widows.) Boida people at the drumming festival recognized Kusnia and Rungo, but everyone by then was drunk and filled with feelings of hail-fellow-well-met, and they all went back to Boida to continue partying. Rungo passed out. Dinarosingh, evidently less fuddled than his companions, sent a message to the police, who came and arrested Rungo and some others. Kusnia escaped but shortly afterwards surrendered. The two outlaw leaders were sent back to jail to serve out their time.

The day after they came out of jail there happened to be a small public ritual being conducted in Boida. Dinarosingh was there; so was the father of Bisipara's Gotikrishna Bisoi, the Warrior who was sirdar of the mutha in which Boida lay. Kusnia and

Rungo and their men descended on the celebrants and beat up Dinarosingh and Gotikrishna's father so badly that the Boida Konds carried them to Bisipara, where there was a dispensary. The next night the outlaws again descended on Boida and set fire to Dinarosingh's house. Since all houses were (and still are) thatched, the entire hamlet was burned out.

Both outlaws were captured the same night. Later they stood trial and were sent, along with some members of their gang, to the Indian penal settlement in the Andaman Islands. Rungo, while in the Andamans, was chronically ill and received a compassionate release before he had served out his time. He returned to the Kondmals, where Ollenbach gave him a humble but steady job as a peon, and he seems to have stayed out of trouble for the rest of his life. Not so Kusnia. He finished his sentence and came home and went on thieving. The Boida Konds laid an ambush and caught him stealing maize. He went to jail again, this time for five years, a long sentence presumably because he was a persistent offender. He was already an old man, and Ollenbach was no longer on the scene. That takes the story into the later 1920s.

When some of the adult males of Boida's Pano street were taken away to the penal settlement in the Andamans, those remaining, mostly older men along with the women and children, were shifted out of Boida and settled in a hamlet built close to the subdivisional headquarters in Phulbani, where, presumably, the police could better keep them under control. The settlement was still there in the 1950s. The Panos resident in Boida in the fifties were not indigenous, both Podo and Lonkera made a point of telling me. They had been imported to be Boida's musicians and to work as laborers for their Kond patrons.

As I write, I have been remembering the way people told me these and other stories and speculating what the manner of telling the tale signifies. I also want to think out what deductions can be made, if it is assumed that the story of Kusnia and Rungo has a framework of fact.

The story was palpably alive more than a quarter of a century after the events took place. Both Podo and Lonkera had the same reason for telling it to me: the difficulty they were having with "their" present Panos. The Bisipara sirdar came out with the story of the night roundup at Katrangia in quite other circumstances, when talking about how his father came to be given the fine, London-made double-barreled shotgun by the sahib (presumably Ollenbach). They—Konds and Oriyas alike—were raconteurs, even the taciturn ones like the Bisipara sirdar. They told all kinds of stories, ranging from when they thought time began to what went on last week or last month here or there in the village or in the Kondmals or sometimes further afield. (I learned of the death of Stalin that way, the teller having heard it from a man in Phulbani market, who heard it from another man, who had been listening to the All-India radio . . . The tale stepped from one teller to another, explaining how each came to be where he was, before we arrived at the death of "their big man.") There is nothing surprising in this fondness for narration. Stories then were still a significant form of entertainment. No one read books; there were no movies, no radios, no televisions; the capacity for losing oneself comfortably in wonder had not been dulled by media sensationalism.

As I said, the sirdar and various other people seemed to enjoy telling me about the exploits of the sahibs. I thought at first they were treating me to a mild and indirect form of flattery, but in fact the tales they told were never consistently in the mode of heroism or nobility. What they said about sahibs usually pointed at something eccentric or bizarre or comical. I have a faint memory of a tale about a sahib who, going out in the garden one night for a pee, stepped on a bamboo rake and was convinced he had been bitten by a snake. Ollenbach's sudden unannounced descents on Bisipara to fine the parents of children who were not in school was, for some reason that I could never grasp, considered funny. Laying in a stock of liquor to capture Kusnia and Rungo has a flavor of the trickster about it. One of Ollenbach's successors was remembered as an indefatigable hunter with an explosive temper. One day the man carrying the sahib's gun,

walking behind him with the weapon casually balanced back-
wards over his shoulder, inadvertently let it off, almost in the
face of the man behind him. Happily, it was a miss. The gun
bearer, in terror of the sahib's rage, dropped the gun and took to
his heels, leaving the unfortunate man who had almost lost his
life standing in the pathway too dazed to move. The sahib, duly
enraged, clouted him. That story was still going the rounds after
twenty years. It could have been told with indignation, framed to
show the Other degraded and humiliated. But it was not; it was
something to laugh about, a manifestation of life's idiocy.

There were other stories into which it is not difficult to read a
political stance and a judgment, including several that have the
mark of ethnic prejudice. Here is part of a text that Lonkera
wrote for me about Olopo Malik, an ancestral hero of the Konds
of this region:

> Olopo Malik was a friend of the king of Boad. One day he asked
> the king for the hand of his daughter. The king said, "You and I
> are two brothers. You cannot marry my daughter. But let us see
> if it is the will of God." So he set tasks for Olopo. The first was
> to split a log, which Olopo did. So the king thought he would
> try a trick. He dressed up his daughter in the clothes of a poor
> woman and on a poor woman he put the raiment of a princess.
> So the Raja said, "Well, Olopo, go on! Seize the one you want to
> marry!" Olopo was taken in; he skipped off with the poor
> woman. All the courtiers laughed and said, "Now we know just
> how clever you are!"
>
> Olopo was covered with shame and in a rage he took the
> woman off into the Kondmals. When he was going along a jun-
> gle path he killed her and cut the meat off her breasts and the
> meat off her thighs and wherever else there was any decent
> meat and took it to the Raja and said, "Great king! I killed a
> sambhar and I am bringing you the gift of some meat."
>
> Some time later he asked the king, "Hey, father-in-law, was
> your daughter's meat good to eat?"

The messages are complicated. Olopo, the Kond, by bidding for
the princess, proclaims himself the equal of the king of Boad, an

Oriya; and yet he is a Kond and the king's subject. (Or perhaps the Boad kings are really Konds.) Olopo is a simple man, easily deceived by the sophisticated raja, but he takes his revenge, visiting a mighty pollution on the raja. The bizarre nature of this revenge clearly gives the story its spice. That the tale is an allegory of Kond-Oriya relationships is also clear; it is, in an ambiguous and complicated fashion, about ethnicity.

A striking feature of the tales about Kusnia and Rungo is the way the two men are featured; they are outlaws and only incidentally Panos. Certainly the story begins with them as thieves, a conventional attribute for a Pano, and it is taken for granted that the maidens' house they visit is Pano. But other possible ethnic associations are not exploited. The story might have highlighted, Robin-Hood-and-his-merry-men fashion, the theme of freedom in the forest (as against drudgery in the fields), or adventure and audacity (characteristics of the highborn not the vassal), or the cunning of the trickster; but none of these is foregrounded. Admittedly, since the tales are told by non-Panos, we would not expect that kind of spin to be put on them. But neither is there any marking of the negative possibilities. Kusnia and Rungo steal, and they beat up those who betray them to the authorities and burn down their houses, but those actions remain embedded in the narrative, inert and unemphasized, not bold, not wicked, but simply what happened. The stories reek of factuality, holding the listeners through the narrative alone—What will happen next?—rather than urging them to find a moral in what took place. These stories are not obvious allegories, as was the tale of Olopo Malik. They are plain narratives. In short, the tales of Kusnia and Rungo survived not because they portrayed anyone's folk heroes, presenting in story form the deep anger of the oppressed, but because their adventures made a good story. I think that is true also of the short-tempered sahib. If there is any quality that holds the stories together (including the fable of Olopo Malik), it is a derisive celebration of humanity, as nonheroic, ridiculous, tricksterlike at best.

Necessity and Rationality

The deduction that might be made from the tale of Kusnia and Rungo—and it may have been lurking at the back of Lonkera's mind when he talked of all those young Pano louts hanging around with nothing to do—is that when Panos become outlaws this could be a sign that the agrarian system has gone awry. Solitary law breakers perhaps point towards deviance, maladjustment in individuals; but gangs of outlaws more clearly advertise something amiss in the working of society. I do not know how things were in the Kondmals at the beginning of the century; I have no information about the frequency of banditry at that time. But it surely could have been the case that conditions then resembled those which Lonkera identified in the 1950s as the cause of Boida's troubles: too many Panos to be supported as farm laborers working for Kond masters.

Social systems are to some extent at the mercy of reproductive chance. Agrarian systems of the kind they had in Bisipara and in Boida work only so long as there is an appropriate balance between the number of masters and the number of servants. If there is a scarcity of workers, then the land is not worked; if there are too many, then someone goes hungry. To a limited extent there can develop a market for labor that balances scarcity in one place with overabundance in another. When the authorities removed Boida's Panos, Podo's forebears imported a new lineage of Panos who, presumably, had not been able to find enough work elsewhere. But agrarian systems cannot by themselves cope with systemwide imbalances.

New production techniques can make up for a shortage of labor. At the other extreme nature by itself, in the form of famine or disease, can solve the problem of too many mouths to feed. The alternative to that cruel solution is the emergence of different economic structures, coexisting with the system of landowning lords and untouchable vassals. Banditry for the Boida Pano was one such alternative; so was theft; so were the Pano looms; so was occasional summer labor for the Public Works Department.

For Bisipara Panos the range was wider: theft (as ever), turmeric trading, cattle dealing, schoolmastering, government jobs, and, most recently for a few confident individuals, a career in politics. The significant element in all these occupations is that they are *not* under the control of the onetime lords of the village, the Konds in Boida and the Warriors in Bisipara.

Panos employed in the alternative economies work for bosses other than their traditional masters. To the degree that this gives them economic freedom, they can also assert a moral independence from those traditional masters, being, so to speak, "individualized out" of the moral obligation that formerly bound master and vassal together. Bisipara's Distillers had a similar experience, once they became rich. They were no longer village servants; they were, quite literally, of independent means.

That experience, I want to stress, can be more than the simple negative feeling of having got out from under a master, the sense that one has escaped from another's control. No less important is the manner in which it is done. Freedom can come in different ways. For example, it can be granted by a superior authority to a category of people; the temple entry legislation is an example. It can also come out of a political struggle, as when India gained its freedom from the British. In both these cases the experience of a new freedom does not highlight anyone's sense of *individual* achievement. On the contrary, the achievement must strengthen the sense of belonging to a collectivity, of being a newly empowered Harijan or a newly liberated citizen of India.

Freedom *as an individual* from a particular master—for example, from a Kond or a Warrior landowner—may be achieved by going into business for oneself. It may also be gained by serving another master, such as the Public Works Department or the weaving cooperative. Inasmuch as these and other government organizations are mainly economic in their idiom, and make no across-the-board moral claims on their employees, those employees, even if they are exploited, yet must gain a sense of themselves as individuals. The relationship is one that encourages self-interest rather than the idea of duty in which the self is lost in devoted service to an institution or a group. Both in the case of Bisipara and of Boida it makes sense to say that villagers could perhaps see themselves, in the Christian idiom, as "of the body," the body being the corporate village. But it would make no sense at all to speak in that way of the Pano weavers who were contracted with the Phulbani cooperative or of the laborers hired seasonally to mend the roads. Raja-praja is a moral relationship, a matter of duty; with the Public Works Department or the weaving cooperative one has only a contract. Raja-praja is a familial idiom; contract is purely economic.

There is another, perhaps more profound, psychological element involved in these experiences. One source for self-respect, even for the awareness of self, is the exercise of knowledge or of skills, the experience of one's own personal encounters with problems that are objectified as things or persons or situations external to the self, and that one resolves by calculating how best to deploy available resources. This is self-respect in the strict sense, not the kind of pride that one might have as a Frenchman, a Catholic, a Brahmin, or a Daughter of the American Revolution. The prime sense of individualism is linked to *homo cogitans*, the rational person standing back and surveying the world outside the self, in order to work out how to make it conform to his or her wishes. *Homo economicus*, the person in search of a living, is a specific kind of *homo cogitans*. Their contrary is *homo hierarchicus*, the unwitting and therefore unprotesting prisoner of duty.[5]

The particular freedoms that in the 1950s Panos claimed in Bisipara—and less sustainedly in Boida—have their origins not in Gandhi's agitation about the Harijans, which was a collective thing, but in generations of experience *as individuals* solving the problem of how to make a living, or part of a living, outside the status of landless, farm-laboring prajas. The presence of the British in the Kond hills during the first half of the nineteenth century had, as that century came to a close, much diversified the

---

[5] The ideal type *homo hierarchicus* is the creation of Louis Dumont (1970).

economy and thereby much increased the scope for Pano enterprise. But even before the British came, the Panos had a rich
experience of living at the margins and living on their wits. Remember Campbell's description: "Panoos . . . transact all business for the Khonds, who consider it beneath their dignity to
barter or traffic, and who regard as base and plebeian all those
who are not either warriors or tillers of the soil." Panos spoke
both the Kui and the Oriya languages, surely a sign of minds
more open to the world than the minds of their masters, the
proudly monolingual Konds. Remember also the function of
these "base and sordid miscreants." Panos went out, presumably
well away from their home territories, to kidnap children and
young adults, who would be raised as meriahs, the victims of
human sacrifice. Neither in ordinary "barter or traffic" nor in
what Campbell saw as criminal adventuring is there room for
attitudes that look for security in the mindless acceptance of a
hierarchy and a collectivity. Traders and kidnappers are thinkers
and calculators, their minds always open to the possibility that
the next transaction might be managed in a different and more
advantageous way.

Such people cannot afford to be part of the herd; their lives are
lived as adversaries. Those who follow the ways of the herd, and
are predictable, are also the losers when they meet opponents
who do not make the obvious moves and do not play the game
by the known rules. A way of life that is deviously nonconform-
ist naturally makes its practitioners unloved by ordinary people.
Still less are they liked by authorities, who much prefer the
mindless conformity of herdlike behavior, characteristic of *homo
hierarchicus*. That is why, in Campbell's writing and almost
throughout the literature, Panos are condemned. It is not that
they were revolutionaries; their failing was a lack of public spirit.
They were not gentlemen; they had not, so to speak, been to the
right schools. In fact, they were simply entrepreneurial individuals, untrustworthy for sure, working out how best, given existing conditions, to serve their own personal interests.

I am coming to the point of arguing that a herdlike mentality, a strong sense of duty to the collectivity, true-believership, altruism towards those privileged as being of the same blood and substance and way of life and faith as oneself—all attributes that are often unthinkingly considered virtuous—are in fact the necessary preconditions for the kind of racism and ethnic or religious prejudice that spins out of control. The pragmatic self-regarding habit of calculating economic advantage, prevalent not only among the Panos but also strong among Oriyas of other castes, is one key to understanding why Bisipara did not descend into outright racism.

To make the case, I shall return in the next chapter to the moral aspects of the God term *Harijan*. This term stands as quite the opposite of the sort of pragmatism I have just been describing. It is a categorical imperative, a value that should not be subjected to cost-benefit calculations.

6

The Sources of Rationality

Discrete Interactions

At least in the very small arenas of Bisipara and Boida, the effect of Gandhi's Harijan campaign was to intensify contempt for untouchables and—a new element in the relationship—to make other people fearful of them because they sometimes seemed to have backers who were both powerful and wrongheaded. Fear makes people irrational and brings with it hatred. That was a paradoxical outcome, since bestowing on untouchables the name *Children of God* was surely intended to make them at least respected, if not loved.

The campaign had this effect because it gave Bisipara's Panos a collective *political* identity, which formerly they did not possess. "Political" in this context means that they became visible as a *group* that was now competing for power in Bisipara. In the old days—at least as the clean castes chose to imagine them—there could have been no such competition, because castes did not compete with one another. Bisipara Panos did have a traditional collective identity, distinct from other castes, but not as a political force. Panos were a caste, dispersed over villages in the Kondmals. The Bisipara segment lived away from the rest of the village in its own street (as did most other castes—Bisipara was an assemblage of ghettos). Its members performed certain functions for the community (farm labor, scavenging, and music making), and consequently Panos had their proper place in the hierarchy of categories that constituted Bisipara's caste system. This place was lowly. With respect to ritual, Panos stood at the margins of the village community because they were excessively unclean, just as the Brahmins, at the other end, being excessively pure, also stood apart. But those same Panos had no traditional group identity as a competitor for political power in the village. In orthodox theory only the Warriors had the privilege and responsibility of exercising power; political competition was supposed to occur only within the Warrior caste between Warriors, never between castes.

Before the Harijan issue surfaced, the occasions when villagers experienced Panos *as a group* could not have been frequent. Music making would be one, especially when villagewide public rituals were performed. The mythology, some of which I have recounted, also sometimes presents Panos as a group, making their own decisions or being subject to the decisions of others. "Panos were not educated," Sindhu wrote. "They did not know how to cultivate for themselves; they always got their food from others." But I suspect the reality then was no different from the common experience of the present (that is, of the 1950s). Harijan issues apart, interaction occurs not between the group of Panos and the group of Warriors or other clean castes but mainly between individuals or individual families in each category. Pano prajas were not vassals of the village; each Pano family was the praja of a particular Warrior family. Insofar as Panos are portrayed in that traditional recollection as having a political life, they had it as individuals (or individual families) who were the clients or retainers of individual Warriors or Warrior families.

The recollection, of course, is not and was not the entire reality, for it speaks only of harmony and cooperation between people of different castes, and it confines conflict and heroics to Warrior adversaries. But harmony or cooperation in a pure form, instant, complete and unnegotiated, is unimaginable. Harmony and cooperation emerge from trial and error, from bargaining and negotiation, which are adversarial processes. The relation of each Bisipara raja, a king, with the praja, his subject, must in every case have been the outcome of continuing offer and counteroffer, a complicated balancing between force and resistance, reward and punishment, imperfectly regulated by a sense of what was right and proper. This is not to say that every morning the Pano went to work pondering ways to screw a better bargain out of his Warrior master, or that he and the master were continually troubled in their consciences about where to draw the line between duty and interest. As everywhere else in social interaction, unthinking habit must have been the major guide. But that unthinking habit itself would have included routinized signaling about where the limits of tolerance would be reached.

In short, everyday experiences through which the Warrior and the Pano, or the Kond and the Pano, came to know one another were experiences between individuals; were, potentially at least, adversarial; were mainly rational, in the sense that the two parties bargained, or at least stood poised to bargain, for an arrangement that would better suit themselves; and were not, when summarized as a relationship, valued intrinsically but *evaluated* for what they would bring or what they would cost.

In correcting the simplistic image of *homo hierarchicus* and a natural harmony between castes, I have made conjectures, from what I observed in the 1950s, about a time for which the same kind of evidence does not exist. No record survives of the tacit dealing that must have gone on between Debohari's great-grandfather and his Pano prajas. Between that time (the mid-nineteenth century) and the 1950s a labor market had emerged and farm labor had become a commodity. Employers compete with one another when the paddy seedlings are transplanted and again, less severely, at harvest time. By the 1950s there were also, to a minor extent, demands for labor in other sectors of the economy.

It might be argued that the very idea of bargaining can only emerge in the context of a free market, and if there was no such market before the 1850s, then perhaps there could not have been tacit bargaining between the master and servant of the kind I saw in the 1950s. I do not think so, because bargaining certainly exists outside the framework of an impersonal marketplace. Every relationship is potentially open to bargaining, including even those in which it is impossible to abandon the connection and enter easily into another one. You cannot shop around for a better mother, but you can bargain with the mother (or with the child) that nature gave you to get a better deal. Thus, in the theory of the raja-praja relationship, the connection is intrinsically valued, very much in the way that a parental relationship is, and cannot normally be terminated in order to gain some extrinsic end. But bargaining to improve the "return" from the relationship (for example by signaling overt or tacit disaffection) must have been possible. Once one gets down to the level of detailing rights and duties (job description, so to speak), the intrinsic quality of any relationship must diminish. Religions (and true believers in one or another sociopolitical ideology) claim that this need not be so and, usually with their own case in mind, that this is not in fact the case; *their* true believers willingly give their *all*. But in practice there is no patterning of behavior that cannot, to some degree, be negotiated, even when the people concerned deny that it is done.

Traditional recollections notwithstanding, the terms of interaction between raja and praja must always have been open to negotiation, although contested to varying degrees at different times, in different places, and between different pairs of actors. But some misgivings remain. While I am sure there were contests, I cannot be certain how much those were in reality contests only *between individuals*. As I noted earlier when describing the imbroglio that arose over the Warrior boy who was pushed into the field, Debohari apparently assumed that it was entirely natural for Panos to react as a brotherhood: "Bali Sahani and all of the brothers will come." Could this spirit not have been abroad in earlier days? Did it never happen that a discontented Pano compared notes with one of his brothers about the deal he had with his Warrior master? Did no Warrior ever look with envy at the industrious Pano who was his neighbor's praja and think about his own lazy retainer? Did Panos never go further and contemplate the equivalent of industrial action, of combining to drive a harder bargain that would benefit them all? At the other end, did it never occur to Warriors that they could, especially since they had a monopoly of force, get more out of their Panos by combining to give them less? In short, could there not have been, in places like Boida and Bisipara, occasions when Panos acted in coordination as a political group (or were seen to do so) long before the word Harijan appeared?

I do not know the answer. The tales of Kusnia and Rungo might be instances of Pano politico-economic mobilization. But no one talked as if they saw Kusnia and Rungo in that light. There are, besides, other reasons to discount earlier collective political mobilization. Some weight certainly must be given to the traditional recollection; the internalized culture, so far as I can ascertain, simply did not entertain political conflict between castes as a possibility. But to rely on that alone, in the present context, would be to beg the question. More persuasive is the argument that collective political action in the form of resistance calls for a collective sense of *intentional deprivation*, that is, a sense that one's present hardship is a price paid for the excessive comfort of another group. But Bisipara's distributive economy, even in the 1950s and surely more so in the past, was mainly a *redistributive economy*. Although Warriors did control the means of production, there was nothing that they could do with any surplus except spread it around. Bisipara had no palaces, no monuments to its ruling group of Warriors, and no more than a minimal investment in the material apparatus of government. In any case, there was never much surplus available. Everyone worked at the same kinds of task, wore similar clothes, and ate the same kind of food. The royal style, to the extent that it existed, was a matter of words and forms of deference, not of conspicuous consumption or architectural magnificence. Material deprivation, when it occurred through failure of the harvest, was an experience for the widest collectivity, for everyone in the village, rulers and subjects alike, not for Panos alone.

Deprivation need not, of course, always take a material form;

one can also be robbed of dignity. Conceivably that, too, could lead to a concerted protest. More often, I suspect, individuals take their own initiatives before humiliation moves them to collective action. The victims, instead of combining with each other to mount a revolution, put their energies into cheating or outwitting their masters in other ways. Thus they diminish their sense of being victimized, both in material terms and in terms of self-respect, because cheating a master or an organization is a way of achieving autonomy. The Panos, indeed, went one step further. In Kond villages they were in effect self-employed as brokers and agents. As Campbell noted, "they transact all business for the Khonds, who consider it beneath their dignity to barter or traffic." In Bisipara, Panos did not have that particular monopoly, but neither were they excluded from the commercial opportunities that were open to the village, especially after the area was pacified.

For these reasons I conclude that, although one cannot absolutely rule out concerted protest in the past, the entry of the Bisipara Panos into the political arena of the village, as a collectivity under the label of Harijan, came as a new experience for everyone, including the Panos themselves. (The village had, of course, already seen a militant caste in action—the Distillers. But, as the conjectures of an earlier chapter suggest, the Distillers probably used the strategy of one-on-one transactions more often than direct collective confrontation.)

Habitual Ethnicity in Bisipara

Since Panos and no one else lived in their own street in Bisipara, since Panos married Panos and no one else, and since the title *Pano* carried with it a characteristic set of images—distinct occupations, dietary habits that others considered revolting, and a greater degree of separation from the divine—it is hard to imagine that Panos were not consistently seen as a distinct category. They had all the markers of being what elsewhere would make them candidates for ethno-racist prejudice. Once again: Why was this prejudice not *politically* salient?

So far, I have answered by pointing out that the relatively even spread of deprivation provided little incentive for collective action by Panos, that Panos did not stand out as suitable scapegoats for this same reason, that Panos were able to exercise individual initiatives on their own behalf, and that Pano political solidarity was decisively crosscut by the discrete relationships between Warrior households and Pano households. These are commonsense answers, and they take for granted that people are rational: they plan and *so far as circumstances will allow* put into practice what *they think* will be best for them.

The cautionary phrases are appropriate. In trying to understand why people behave the way they do, there is a constant temptation to give more weight to calculation than is realistic. We, the observers, usually with the benefit of hindsight, calculate the consequences of a particular course of action and then assume that the actor must have made the same calculations. Even when people do things that any sane person knows will hurt them, we take refuge in the concept of unconscious motivation, assuming that some simulacrum of means/end calculation has gone on in response to, say, a death wish or the guilt feelings precipitated by an Electra complex. But, as is everyone's introspective experience, action is often triggered not by direct calculation of its consequences but simply by identifying, almost unreflectively, a particular context that habitually goes with the action. We sort out a classroom, a party, a tête-à-tête, or an encounter with a policeman and conduct ourselves accordingly, without ever systematically surveying the consequences of doing what is inappropriate. That kind of unreflective knowledge is a key to understanding how the Panos stood in the past and how the perception of them began to change once they were called Harijan. The use of that label, together with the legislation that went with it, began to bring Pano status out of the unreflective mode into an arena of disputation.

Unreflective, habitual action is not, by definition, the product of an ideology. Ideologies are articulated and defended or attacked. They represent heightened forms of intellectual and emotional awareness, which are absent from habitual action. The actors involved, so long as they act out of habit, do not question the rightness or wrongness of what they are doing: they simply do it. Strange though it may sound, I think that the frame of mind in which Bisipara people dealt with all caste differences, not just the divide between untouchables and the rest, came near to that level of unreflective unconcern.

It does sound strange because everyone in Bisipara made a parade of being quite meticulous in observing rules about marriage, acceptance of food, place of residence, bodily contact, right of access to specified places, and all the other minutiae of a life organized by the caste system. It also sounds strange because, as one would expect, when matters were brought out of the realm of habit into the arena of ideology where opinions are disputed, those opinions were strongly held and seemed likely to provoke violent action. But as one looks more closely at the scene, certain features emerge that perhaps indicate an underlying lack of concern for, and occasionally even skepticism about, the importance of caste differences. Certainly Bisipara people did not tolerate departures from habitual proprieties with respect to caste residence, interdining, or marriage rules. But neither did they live in everyday dread of such things happening. They were not constantly on the lookout for actions or events that might be the thin end of a wedge that would prize open the door to chaos. They did not seem to feel, in other words, that the underlying order was under threat; there was no reason to fear those who were different and therefore no cause to be impassioned. The attitude I am trying to describe is well portrayed by the Warrior who said, "Who are we Warriors? They say we are Ksattriyas, but we are not. We are just Konds who happened to come out on top." He laughed, seemingly amused by the thought.

I have in mind the contrast between that relaxed attitude and the strong emotions that go with the presence of blacks in white-dominated countries, or of Jews at certain times in Christian countries, or of Gypsies everywhere. Bisipara's "others," as groups, are certainly ethnically differentiated in a variety of ways. They are seen literally as distinct breeds; they have distinct customs, and interaction with others must be closely regulated for fear of contamination. But India and Hinduism are unique in the combination of features that mark their style of discrimination. First, as I said, in Bisipara and most other places in India, no one caste stands out as a minority because every caste is a minority. Second, society (in the form of the caste system) integrates multiple minorities and gives them legitimate standing; plurality is the norm. That is not a situation in which minorities are considered an undesirable appendage, something that should be excised from the body politic to make it healthy. Bisipara's Panos had their legitimate place in the social hierarchy, as did everyone else. Third, Bisipara is not the plural society of J. S. Furnivall (1948), in which different ethnic groups, mutually tolerant, sometimes equal sometimes not, exist within the controlling framework of a dominant colonial state. The Hindu community's social fabric is held together not simply by the concentration of power in a government but also by a division of functions between its different ethnicities and by the largely unreflective and widespread assumption that this is how the world works and how it should work.

In short, ethnicity in Bisipara, by its very pervasiveness, was taken for granted, and until recently it remained below the threshold of ideological debate. It was not an ideology to be argued and defended; it was simply an ethos, a way of life that people followed. They were not driven to be impassioned about it, since it was not under overt and organized challenge. There was no challenge because people were hardly aware of the system, certainly never thinking to weigh it against alternative designs for living. In any case, they were mostly busy making a living.

Of course, there had always been the tacit challenge that existed because individuals to some extent were "self-employed," not entirely dependent on their place in the caste system to support themselves. The Pano entrepreneurs had always been somewhat independent, able to keep a part of their lives free from the dictates and intrusions of their masters. No Kond ever told his Pano how and where to kidnap a meriah victim. No Warrior ever told his praja precisely how to dispose of the carcass of the ox that died. Perhaps these areas of discretion are better described not as a challenge to ethnic domination but simply as marking the limits of its applicability.

A second form of challenge, somewhat more direct, is exemplified by the story of the Distillers. They too became their own economic masters. But when they mounted a challenge it was not to the system but to their position within it. They set out to negotiate themselves a more respectable place in the caste hierarchy. In doing this they were simply following one of the unspoken pragmatisms of the caste system (or, indeed, of any hierarchy): rank tends eventually to level itself with power (which in this case was derived from wealth). The changes that their efforts produced, which were cumulative, were often discreet, quite near to the unreflective mode of interaction that I described earlier. Certainly in the 1950s there was very little moral posturing, very little drama, nothing comparable in scale and publicity to the Harijan campaign.

A third type of challenge is exemplified by that campaign, which began to redefine the rules for competition in Bisipara's political arena.

The Nature of Moral Feelings

It is a feature both of Hinduism and of Christianity that spiritual goodness does not sit easily with material wealth. "God's mercy is infinite; it will save even a rich man," said Anatole France. Many Brahmins in India (though not in Bisipara) are rich and fat, but an esteemed figure in popular culture is the "poor Brahmin." In Bisipara it was taken for granted that wealth is never honestly come by; riches and virtue are in complementary distribution, and a life of material self-denial, as an ascetic, is a virtuous life. Nowhere is that better illustrated than in the much-publicized lifestyle and the philosophy of Mahatma Gandhi.

Asceticism was understood in Bisipara as a form of holiness, but Gandhi's humanist philosophy would for sure have been caviare to the villagers' general unreflective predispositions. The people there would not have appreciated it. They did not, at least in my hearing, ever discuss generalized humanism; but if they had been invited to think about their own Panos in those terms—all people are the same, all morally equivalent—they would surely have been bemused.

Bisipara villagers were, from time to time, invited to come near that condition. Once, about six years after Gandhi had been murdered, the Phulbani Harijan inspector made them aware of Vinoba Bhave's *Bhoodan*, a Gandhian-style scheme for donating land that would then be distributed among landless untouchables. As I said, they fantasized a dusty answer for him ("Let them give us some land!"), while in fact registering very clearly in their minds the inspector's threat to fine them huge sums for even using the word *untouchable*.

What Gandhi stood for, on almost every count Bisipara people stood against. Mostly they were unaware that they did so. Gandhi for them was what he was, I suspect, for most humble people in India, a remote saintlike figure who, they had heard, did good things. They did not know exactly what these things were, nor did it matter much. A saint was judged for what he was and how he lived, not for what he accomplished. A saint was a saint, a holy man, somehow in touch with the divine, and Gandhi was a bigger and better version of their own Sankaro Bisoi, a young unmarried man who dressed in saffron cloth and was Lord Krishna's devotee. (He was a distant cousin of Jaya and Debohari.) Other conspicuously pious people, of whom they had experience, they judged false. Sindhu Sahani, as I said, they thought to be no more than a canting scoundrel. They took a particular delight in telling me of another self-proclaimed holy man, a "babaji," a Harijan who had come to enlighten the people

of Panosai and had been seen endeavoring to have carnal knowledge of a she-buffalo—it was a scandal, they said happily. They
called a meeting and confronted him with witnesses, and when
he offered to take an oath that the story was false, they found
technicalities to prevent him from clearing his name that way.
But, they knew for sure, there were genuine saints, and it was a
way of life that, in principle, Bisipara people admired.

Withdrawal and asceticism they respected, but they did not
count as authentic those saints who were politically active (unaware or perhaps unwilling to acknowledge that Mahatma Gandhi fell into that category). Genuine saints, who were teachers,
taught people a kind of personal redemption, a way to save
themselves, and that was acceptable. But teaching new ways to
see the world and trying to change the order of society were not
acceptable. So the Harijan inspector, even if he did spend a lot of
time in prayer, came out of their scrutiny more or less as an
interfering and unrealistic politician or official (as I said, I suspect that in fact he was a social worker in the Gandhian style).

Had the people of Bisipara been able to make articulate their
own unreflective philosophy, the principles that guided their everyday interactions with one another, and had they then been
informed of what Gandhi's philosophy contained, they would
surely have seen a point-by-point contradiction. Gandhi saw the
essential caste system to be an arrangement of coordinate groups
that maintained their distinctiveness but shared a common humanity, which made it natural that they would cooperate harmo-
niously with one another for the common good. Bisipara people,
on the other hand, knew that power was differentially distributed between castes, and they never thought things could be otherwise. There were, always had been, and always would be
rulers and their subjects.

Gandhi's vision of the natural social world was an ordering of
groups—villages and castes—not an ordering of individuals. Accordingly, true freedom for the individual, in that often-used
paradox, is achieved only when individuals surrender their purported interests to the needs of society. At one level, Bisipara

people thought that way too, conceptually enfolding individuals into families, castes, and villages. But at another level they lived out a different conception altogether, one that comes quite near to our notion of the rational individual or of economic man. This was the concept of a person who cares for his own interests before concerning himself with his duties to caste, to village, or sometimes even to family, and who certainly never thinks about obligations to mankind at large.

Economic man is occupied with material things. Gandhi's moral man directs himself towards spiritual ends, and he concerns himself with material things only as a means to spiritual ends (which most commonly means rejecting material comforts). In fact, such a person largely dispenses with the means/end framework as a tool for calculation. The first question is not "What will be the consequences of this action?" but rather "Is this action morally good in itself?" Ends never justify means. If an action is seen as a means to an end, it must, before being used, first pass the test of its own intrinsic rightness.

Gandhi, of course, is not unique in employing this style of reaching decisions. True believers everywhere behave that way. If asked, as Gandhi sometimes was, how he knew what was right from what was wrong, what was true from what was false, his answer was that truth will be intuitively known. It might not be instantly known, and "what appears to be truth to one may appear to be error to another." Resolution is achieved when, it seems, one or the other gives way: "pursuit of truth [does] not admit of violence being inflicted on one's opponent but he must be weaned from error by patience and sympathy" (quoted in Bondurant 1965, 16–17).

My present concern is not with the validity of these assertions but rather with the frame of mind that they indicate. It has three characteristics. First, it goes beyond rationality, being unconcerned with means and ends and doing no more than assert that some ends are "true" (in other words, desirable or morally imperative) and others are "in error." Second, despite the insistence on nonviolence and despite the gentleness connoted by "weaned" and "patience and sympathy," the situation envisaged is essentially adversarial (note the word "opponent"). Third, it makes no room for compromise and bargaining. It is not the case that I must trade away a little of my "truth" in exchange for what you will abandon from your "truth." Truth remains whole and entire, indivisible and nonnegotiable, and when it is encountered it will (eventually) be recognized. It does not require much reflection, and no more than a brief look at the way Gandhi himself conducted his political life, to realize that this is the strong-arm style of negotiating for "truth." The person whose ideas are "in error" is the one who blinks first.

This is the Pandora's box that the term *Harijan* represented for Bisipara's Warriors and the rest of the clean castes. The word invited them to think critically about the way their social system had hitherto worked, to accept that it was in error, and to change it. They were invited to see their Panos as a group, a group that had been unjustly deprived of its rights, a group that was now to be privileged as a group and as the Children of God. The individuals who had once been someone's praja, or a day laborer, or one of the village watchmen, or a schoolmaster, could retain those identities, but only secondarily because as individuals they would now be marked by the dominating identity of Harijan. The bargaining and negotiating and adjusting of discrete relationships that had formerly gone on under one or another of those terms (praja, watchmen, and the rest) were now liable to be skewed and standardized by the nonnegotiable attribute *Harijan*. That attribute mobilized the Panos as contenders for political power in Bisipara.

For sure, warriors and the other clean castes did not acknowledge the moral clout that was purportedly contained in the Harijan label. But in fact more than morality was involved. Despite Gandhi's version of how the world ought to work, the Harijan program only went forward when driven by external force, in other words, when pushed by politicians and the government.

Pervasive Pragmatism

Moral fervor—the kind that does not count the cost of action and insists that, come what may, "truth" must prevail—was noticeably absent from everyday behavior in Bisipara. Certainly an outsider might say, with Wordsworth, that the world was too much with them. But in fact they were less concerned with getting and spending than with surviving, with doing what had to be done. They were intelligent, feeling people, but with a strong and solid sense of what was practical.

Much of their life was suffering, and they did not for a moment think they were living in a paradise that needed no fixing. My notes are full of stories of misfortune: cattle dying, people dying and the cost of funerals, a quiverful of daughters and the ruinous cost of marrying them off, children dying when they had survived long enough to be known and loved, sickness, sometimes hunger, and a great array of hardships not known in more affluent societies. They also knew of injustice, how those with power abused others, and sometimes when they saw a remedy they went for it. They deplored enmities that occurred where they should not, between fathers and sons, husbands and wives, or brothers. They also, despite the prevailing commercial ethos, managed to combine with it a public insistence on duty to one's family and community; wealth was not the only thing they valued. Nor were they merely cold calculators. They had feelings and emotions, as does everyone, and they sometimes acted impetuously, out of love or in a rage.

What they did not have was the Gandhian moral fervor, the deep conviction that the world could be made a better place if everyone became a better person. They were not into moral conversions on the grand scale, certainly not into those that would fundamentally change the form of their community. Change and improvement in itself was not unthinkable. They knew of personal salvation, as when a man renounced the world and became a sannyasin. Some of them, also, were forthrightly ambitious about improving their worldly lives, which in effect meant making money and acquiring property or securing a government job. But they did not think about serving a cause and were not drawn to those who proposed sacrifice for the public good. In the first half of the 1950s they taxed themselves to rebuild a better temple for Sri Ramchandro—and unceasingly accused one another of embezzling the funds. In those same years they were being bombarded with community development plans, and they looked constantly for the private vices that they thought were being served behind the facade of public benefits. Their motto could have been Cicero's *Cui bono* (Who has a piece of the action?). The great cause of their lifetime—India's struggle for freedom from Britain—had mostly happened over the horizon. There were no "freedom fighters" in Bisipara, none, so far as I know, in the Kondmals. At that time (the 1950s) to have been a freedom fighter was usually a passport to success for assembly candidates in the coastal districts of Orissa. Bisipara's constituency returned a former raja, not a freedom fighter. (A few men in government employ told me they had thought it prudent to vote "for the raj"—they meant the ruling Congress party—but they had instructed their wives to vote the family's conscience by supporting the Raja of Kalahandi.)

I do not imply that Gandhi stood alone on that pinnacle of moral intensity. In the 1950s there were many people in Orissa who were visionaries: politicians, social workers, and (rarely) officials. I first went there only five years after the British were expelled from India, a time when the public stage was still dominated by the heroes of the freedom fight. "Bliss was it in that dawn to be alive . . ." could well be said of their demeanor, not because they were reliving the recent victory but because most of them were still looking with confidence to the future, to the immense task of making a nation and a good society, and they were confident of their ability, now that the imperial power had gone, to create such a society. They were still carried forward by the freedom fight's spirit of unquestioning self-sacrifice. In the freedom fight they had submerged themselves and their individual interests in the movement, and at that time they *knew* without a doubt that everything was possible for those who truly believed and were ready to sacrifice themselves for the cause. Watching them, talking privately with them, hearing them tell the story of their lives, I think I understood what it meant to be a true believer.

It did not last. Between 1952 and 1955, when I first lived in Bisipara, I did not have much contact with public figures, and much of what I have just written comes from 1959, when I spent a year talking with Orissa's politicians and officials. At that time there was still much public enthusiasm. People seemed still to be confident that they could shape their future, and despite emerging differences (as between Gandhians and those more concerned with the practicalities of planning, or between socialists and others more to the right) they still believed that effort would get its due reward and that much indeed had already been accomplished in the twelve years of freedom. They also still found it convenient to blame whatever failures were then becoming apparent on the legacy of imperialism.

That was the public face. In private, here and there, I began to hear a different tale. It came mostly from those who had been active in the freedom fight—they were now in or approaching middle age. Age, for sure, touches up the past and hides its blemishes, but in this case I think their memories were not playing tricks: the lost virtues that they lamented really had once existed and had now vanished. One after another I heard them speak of the growing venality of present-day government and politics. Mostly they spoke with sadness, occasionally with anger, and always seeming perplexed that a moral climate could change so quickly. They were not referring to the day-to-day petty administrative corruption that was endemic; that could be blamed on the way the British structured the lower echelons of the civil service. What disturbed them was a higher moral failing: increasingly, it seemed, political leaders, even some of those who had distinguished themselves for their selflessness in the freedom fight, were out to serve themselves, not the movement or the cause. After 1947 they behaved as if the time had come to enjoy the spoils. Institutions served by such men could not but fail, people said, and the current optimism about the future and about building the good society was surely unfounded. Indeed, it was no longer agreed what shape the good society should take.

A clear intellectual and practical refuge for those who felt this disenchantment was one or another version of the Gandhian philosophy. The late Nabakrushna Chaudhuri, who had been the chief minister of Orissa's Congress government in 1952 when I first arrived there, retired from party politics sometime in the 1950s to work for Vinoba Bhave's *Bhoodan* movement. Eventually he built an ashram in Angul district as a base for social work among tribal peoples. I saw him there in the late 1970s and talked with him, an old and frail man, still with enthusiasm and still without anger. For him, as for any Gandhian, large-scale institutional engineering intended to compel right conduct was not the pathway to the good society. Things worked the other way around: the morality that inheres in human nature must be allowed to take the lead, and the good society would then emerge of its own accord.

The small cloud of private disillusion I saw in 1959, which would later grow into a pervasive public cynicism, was quite predictable. Moral fervor thrives on simplicity. It flourishes in a world where right and wrong are transparently different and instantly recognizable, where there is no compromise and no concession, no ambiguity and no uncertainty. That, of course, can seldom be a real world; and when it is, the result is likely to be disaster. More often it is an imagined world created with the help of a God term. *Swaraj* (self-rule) was the reigning God term up to and beyond 1947; freedom from the British was all that mattered. That, for many Indians, was their imagined world, a one-dimensional world with everything clearly marked as good or evil. (That also was the kind of Manichean world—the saved set against the unsaved, the washed against the unwashed—that the God term *Harijan* might have created for the people of Bisipara had they not been too busy struggling to survive life's everyday assaults.)

After 1947 the God term *Swaraj* began to lose its magic. Its enchantment evaporated because once freedom had been attained, people had to unwrap the bundle labeled "freedom" and decide what, of the many things it contained, they really wanted. They also had to decide how to get what they wanted. They also had to decide who they were, because members of what once had been a united team fighting against the imperialists now found themselves in an arena where former comrades fought against each other. The situation, in short, was no longer conducive to moral fervor. As it had always been in the village, so now, in the 1950s and increasingly afterwards, practicality became a habit also on the national scene. People had learnt to count up costs and benefits and to ask, cautiously and skeptically, who would benefit and who would pay the cost.

Counting the cost and the cautiously rational conservatism that goes with it were tried and trusted procedures among officials and administrators. Individual administrators, particularly those who made a mark, did often have enthusiasms. I met some, particularly younger men, who were zealots for community development. British administrators, too, had their visionaries. Philip Woodruff's two books on the British in India, *The Founders* and *The Guardians*, especially the second, abound with examples. In the Kondmals Ollenbach had literacy as his hobbyhorse. But for the most part the civil servant's motto could have been, with Tacitus, *sine ira et studio*, "without anger or zeal." The reason again is obvious: anger and zeal are poor tools for coping with details. I vividly recall the low-key contempt that Vinoba Bhave's campaigns aroused in a senior civil servant. Vinoba and his people, he said, were mostly makers of chaos, because Vinoba "on the march" never gave a thought to the logistics of his forays, to the costs of security, to the resources that did not go where they were needed because Vinoba had preempted them, or even to the administrative tangles that followed from unplanned land redistribution and uncertain land titles. The officials lived in perpetual disenchantment because it was their job to count the costs of moral fervor.

In such an atmosphere anyone who parades a true belief runs the risk of being thought not only unrealistic and irresponsible and immature but also hypocritical. That was the judgment the Bisipara people passed on the Harijan inspector. That was also how the local officials understood the intervention by the politicians who visited the Boida ashram school. Perhaps, in the end, that would have been how the ministers judged themselves: they may have seen themselves as doing no more than what was politically expedient. The officials, going so carefully by the book when they made their inquiries, were doing what it would be impolitic not to do; they were concerned at best with due process and, for sure, were not primarily moved by a moral concern for what might have been called *Harijanism*.

Although neither side in Bisipara was guided in its conduct by the Harijan movement, because they did not accept its philosophy, both did make use of it. There was a whiff of true belief. The Pano leaders, on public occasions and when it suited them to do so, spoke the language of moral fervor; so too did the Warriors and the other clean castes, once they began to be a little afraid of what might happen. Rampant ethnic hatreds, of the kind now associated with the phrase "ethnic cleansing," seemed to be at least a possibility. But in fact this true belief, although of the kind that elsewhere might have become a thunderstorm, in Bisipara floated like a cloud in the sky above harvesters, enough to make them anxious but not enough to stop them getting on with the necessary tasks of everyday life.

In the next chapter I will argue that the cataclysm was averted because, first, rational calculations of relatively personal advantage still dominated the scene, especially among the Panos, and, second, the institutional arrangements were such that normal rational effort mostly paid off, whereas mindless enthusiasm and violent action would not have.

7

The Bottom Line

The Quiet Revolution

It is thirty-five years since I last stayed in Bisipara. There must still be Warriors alive who garrisoned the Sibhomundiro to keep the Panos out, and others, some years later, who attended the second officer's court in Phulbani to hear the Pano litigation withdrawn. Perhaps also, on the other side, Pano leaders—Sindhu the schoolmaster, Gondho the former policeman who became secretary of the statutory village council, and other prominent men—still remember the 1950s and recall how in those days they did things that no Pano had done before. Sindhu has built a temple; Gondho and Balunki have stood as candidates for a seat in Orissa's legislature; about 1957 Gondho became the appointed secretary of the newly constituted village council. Perhaps they remember; but I cannot imagine any of them thinking back and saying to themselves (and therefore saying it sincerely), "Bliss was it in that dawn . . ." Freedom-fighting politicians may have positioned themselves in that light in the early 1950s, as I suggested, but surely not Bisipara people. The nearest anyone in Bisipara ever came to manning a barricade was in those two damp-squib incidents described earlier, hardly moments of glory, mere sparks that quickly fizzled out when the bureaucrats turned on their sprinklers. Yet I believe that I was, in the 1950s, witnessing a revolution in Bisipara.

On the day of the full moon in the month of Srabono, which in 1953 fell on August 24, the people of Bisipara hold a festival. They honor the god Balaram, the elder brother of Krishna. Balaram, Debohari explained, was born holding a plough in his hand, and the plough was one of the weapons he used to slay his enemies. They call the festival *Goma Purnomi* (Mother Cow's full moon). As Debohari wrote,

> Almost everyone had finished planting by this date and there was rejoicing. The day before people went around looking for goat meat to buy, as much they were able, some a rupee's worth, some two rupees' worth. The Panos ate pork. Non-meat-eaters went to the shop and bought molasses and coconuts to make cakes.
>
> In the morning every cultivator sticks a branch of *kendu* in a paddy field, to keep off the evil eye.[1] Some say it is to deter insects. Many do not know the reason but plant the branch anyway because they see their neighbors doing it.

Debohari continued at length, explaining how the cattle are not yoked that day but sent out with the Herdsman to graze in the forest, and how, when the cattle return in the evening, they are anointed with ghi, fed medicinal herbs to make them strong, and given a token handful of cooked rice, the remainder of the dish going to the Herdsman. Later in the day Trinatho Bisoi, the Warrior who served as *dehuri* (priest) for the village's tutelary deity (Komeswari), performed a ritual and invested the deity with a sacred thread. The men then assembled in the meeting house, and Oruno the Brahmin placed a sacred thread on all of them in turn, the purpose being to protect everyone from the attentions of a demon who "gobbles up men of all castes except the Brahmins." Everyone became an honorary Brahmin for the day. In return each household made Oruno a gift of uncooked rice (*caulo*).

In the early afternoon of August 24, after the midday meal had

---

[1] The tree is ebony, *Diospyros melanoxylon*. Its leaves are used to wrap bidis, the Indian cigarettes.

Goma jumping in 1953. This was a demonstration for my benefit by one of those who had just built the gantry. The festival began later in the day.

been eaten, festivities began. The day before, young men—all clean-caste—had built a ramp of earth in the middle of Warrior street, three or four yards long and rising to about four feet high. Some distance ahead of this they put up a bamboo gantry, the crossbar being, as I remember, about twelve feet from the ground. From this bar they hung small prizes contributed by the shopkeepers of the village—combs, mirrors, cone-shaped packets of bidis, soap, betel nut, and various cheap trinkets. The game was to run up the ramp (which they also called goma) and hurl oneself through the air, attempting to snatch a prize from the crossbar. First the dehuri (Komeswari's priest) jumped. He was a middle-aged man, and, like a politician throwing out the first ball at a baseball match, he made no more than a token effort. Then the young men tried. "Many failed," Debohari wrote. "Sudro Bisoi did best. Some youths sprained wrists or ankles, jumping badly." Later they lowered the bar and brought it nearer to the ramp and gave small boys their turn. One by one the trinkets were taken. When they had all gone, the crowd wandered away. I sat nearby talking with someone, and I noticed two or three Panos, small boys, jumping from the ramp, trying their skill at reaching the bar. By then no prizes were left.

I saw no sign of Panos while the rituals were going on, but when the jumping competition began many Panos—men, women, and children, all sitting together on the north side of the ramp—joined in the cheering and laughter that accompanied the jumps and the falls. (People especially enjoyed the clowning of two older men who lumbered ponderously up the ramp and then lowered themselves cautiously from its end.) I failed to ask what else the Panos did on that day. I assume that in their own fields and their own homes they did more or less what others did, planting the kendu branch and indulging their cows and oxen.

I saw Goma Purnomi again in 1955. The performance was exactly the same, Panos watching, no young Panos competing, even Sudro Bisoi still doing well. I saw it again four years later in 1959 when I spent a few weeks in Bisipara. The setting was the same: a ramp built in Warrior street just to the east of the meeting house, a gantry, and small packages hanging from it. In earlier years people had made sure I knew what was going on, so that I would be there to see the fun and make a contribution to the expense. But in 1959, although I had been a few days in the village, no one had mentioned Goma Purnomi. I just happened on the festival, walking to Jodu Bisoi's post office, which was on the north side of the street, adjacent to the ramp. Jodu was sitting on his verandah and watching, with noticeable indifference, what was going on. No other Warrior adult—or adult of any clean caste—was present. A few clean-caste boys—not youths but children—were taking part. I sat down beside Jodu to watch, and after a time he asked rhetorically, "Who are the rajas now?" and answered, "Not us!"

The man who seemed to be raja for the day was that same Gondho Sahani, the one-time policeman, assembly candidate, and presently secretary of the statutory village council. He dominated, now barking out orders like the policeman he had been, now chivying on small boys as a scoutmaster might do, coming across to greet me (and ignoring Jodu), and returning to crack jokes with the audience, who, so far as I could see, were all Panos. The competitors were by now small children, and a few of those who jumped were from clean-caste households. The older competitors, standing around and sharing out the bidis they had won, were all Pano youths.

I had other things to do that year and had come to Bisipara mostly for a holiday, and regrettably I did not follow up on that scene, which is all that exists in my notes and in my memories. The scene is still vivid. I remember that Gondho was wearing shoes, as were several other Pano men. Some wore bush jackets and long trousers. Standard village turnout was bare feet, sandals at most (in August, when there is still a good deal of water about, most people preferred to go barefoot), a dhoti, and on formal occasions a long, side-pocketed shirt. Even more surprising was the sight of several young Pano matrons in cholis (blouses) and long saris, with faces rouged and powdered, and—I saw one instance—wearing high-heeled shoes. At the beginning of the decade village women did not wear cholis, not even on festive occasions, and they always went barefoot, and make-up was limited to eye lining, the dot on the forehead, and sometimes a slash of vermilion in the hair parting.

Had I thought to follow up on this scene, which so much astonished me, I would have asked Jodu or Debohari or Jaya whether clean castes performed the rest of the day's rituals—the kendu branch in the fields, anointing the cattle, bestowing the sacred thread, and the rest. I assume they did, and that the sacred part of the day's work—celebrating Balaram, his plough, the cattle, and the wealth that the earth brought them—must have been notionally separated from the goma jumping, which they now sequestered into a political arena, so to speak, and abandoned to the Panos, the political victors (who then had the effrontery to stage the affair in Warrior street). I would also like to have found out how and why there had been such a change, how the decisions were made, and how the Warriors and other clean castes rationalized their boycott. I suspect—again I do not know—that sometime during those four intervening years young Pano men must have presented themselves as competitors for goma jumping, perhaps inviting (or threatening to invite) the Harijan inspector, or promising to make a complaint to the courts if they were excluded as untouchables. Perhaps also Gondho's office, as the salaried and appointed secretary to the government-approved and elected statutory panchayat, gave the Warriors a way to rationalize the Pano takeover. If the goma jumping had been bought out by the government, that would be one more reason for village people not to put their energies into it.

I sat there having a disconnected conversation with Jodu for no more than half an hour. The scene has remained vivid because it (and Jodu's comment) marked clearly and dramatically a stage in Bisipara's slow emergence into a more open society. It signified—albeit at the level of seedling—a revolution, the passing of the caste system as the organizing framework of Bisipara's community and the birth of a new form, the political equivalent of the marketplace, where the prizes go to those who are quick to seize their opportunities and who are more concerned to advance their interests than to see duty performed.

But the matter was more complicated than that. It might not have been so if a small, caste-based community could move directly into an open society in which all citizens are equal. But such a move would be possible only if all existing loyalties and prejudices, all existing hierarchy and all memory of it, could be instantly erased, which is clearly an impossibility. New forms of interaction may be legislated, but old customs and old habits of thought remain. Indeed, more than thought remains, because without total erasure of the past culture, those previously underprivileged (in this case untouchables) start with a disadvantage.

Fairness, then, requires that they be compensated. But what kind of open society is it that favors and privileges a particular social category? The paradox is the same one that embarrasses all societies when, moved by guilt or apprehension, they endeavor to make amends for past inequities. At least in the short run, to make people equal it is necessary to give some of them special advantages, thus perpetuating and sometimes intensifying inequality, albeit reversing the previous order of privilege. In short, to be called Harijan is, de facto, to be privileged; not to be Harijan is to carry a handicap. Bisipara's clean castes were never slow to point this out.

The matter also is complicated because it pays the smart, self-interested competitor in the political marketplace to make use of such morally enjoined inequalities. There may then be a quadruple thrust towards emotion-driven conflict. Some people will accept the intransigent morality of the true-believing Gandhi as an imperative to be obeyed without counting the cost, and they will be matched and fought by those who have the opposite faith. Others, more cynical, act in the same way and follow the same strategy not because they believe it is morally right but because they see advantages in doing so. There will also be opportunists who, without posturing as moralists themselves, make cynical use of others' moral fervor.

Thus, one way or another, a premium is offered to those who take a step in the direction of irrationality. It pays the Panos (or so it seems) to assert their moral standing as Harijans. When they do so, they not only proclaim their own unwillingness to compromise but also drive their opponents, the Warriors and the other clean castes, into a matching irrationality that defines the conflict as one between different kinds of creature, between whom rational communication and therefore compromise are impossible.

From the Warriors' point of view things in Bisipara had certainly fallen apart. The center, which was supposed to hold so that things would stay in place, was the caste hierarchy; it put Warriors in charge of the social world. They did not, so far as I saw, take the change gracefully. They lost no chance to denigrate Panos, as the brief excerpts from Debohari's texts show, and when they spoke the word "Harijan," they used the tone of voice that Americans of the mindless right once used for communists and now reserve for "liberals" (seemingly unaware that liberal-ism once enshrined individual liberty and free markets). But at the same time Bisipara's Warriors did not organize death squads, nor even go in for Nixon-style underhandedness. Mostly they got on with their daily lives and were able to limit prejudice to performances on the political stage, almost, it sometimes seemed, to playacting. They cooperated with Panos when it seemed to be advantageous. During that same short visit in 1959 I saw a joint delegation of the leading clean-caste men of the village, along with Sindhu and Gondho and Balunki (the Congress constituency agent), all three of them Panos, hasten to a nearby crossroads to intercept a touring minister. They were carrying a petition to get their Upper Primary school elevated to the category of Middle English. In short, both sides were quite pragmatic about their differences, not in the least religiously fanatical, as one might have expected. Everyone, in the end, kept cool; there was no failure of nerve.

So far, I have explained this common sense, this prudent lack of mindless fanaticism, by saying that Bisipara's life style was such that people there were accustomed to calculating utility, weighing the consequences of what they proposed to do. Now, in the rest of the chapter, I will describe certain counterforces that might have undermined this pragmatism and driven people—under Gandhi's inspiration, ironically—to a genocidal hatred of the extreme kind that is seen not only in the rest of the world but also in India, both between its two major religions and within Hinduism itself.

The Culture of Moderation

Moderation and calculation flourish when people remain confident that effort will have at least some of its due reward and they can work through existing institutions to keep their lives short of being intolerable. Of course this does not mean that they believe everything is perfect; it means only that they are not fundamentally unnerved, deprived of strength, and reduced to fearfulness, waiting for a miracle to save them or a leader to perform the miracle.

Neither Warriors nor Panos nor anyone else in Bisipara suffered from such a failure of nerve. Life in Bisipara in the 1950s, compared to the life that I lived in Britain (even in immediate postwar Britain), was very harsh. People sometimes went hungry. They died of diseases that (I knew) were medically preventable. One year the rains at first failed and then came in such abundance that some bottom-lying paddy fields seemed likely to be swept away (fortunately they were not, although the newly planted seedlings in them were lost). But as I made clear earlier, although some people were relatively rich and many others were poor, all were more or less indifferently exposed to the risks that nature put upon them. In the traditional structure, there were rulers and ruled, but the rulers were not conspicuously better off than those they ruled. I believe this had always been the case, and it became even more so when the sharp politico-economic division between masters and servants (between Warriors and the rest) became blurred by the quiet revolution that Macpherson, Campbell, and others unknowingly brought to the Kondmals. Nor was there the kind of general decline in living standards that makes people conscious of deprivation, of how much better off they had been in the past. Bisipara's living memory had no trace of a golden age; life had always been this way—tough, sometimes miserable, but for the most part endurable.

Underneath the posturing, the almost contrived anger and staged anxiety, and despite the occasional impetuous and obviously unconsidered act, people were mostly phlegmatic. They saw no fundamental threat to their way of life; indeed, they took care not to threaten it. Boida Konds were foolish enough to propose depriving themselves of the labor force they needed in their fields. Bisipara people, not so stupid, confined their punitive ventures to getting themselves a new set of musicians, thereby depriving the offenders of the occasional handout that was the privilege of a village musician. Even the Boida people came to their senses fast enough, and as soon as the hot season ended and work in the fields awaited, they conveniently forgot what they had pledged themselves to do.

It is true that the standard Warrior posture was one of despair. "Who are the rajas now?" Jodu asked. It is also true that their public attitude to Panos was routinely adversarial; they never acknowledged in words that Panos were in some ways useful, even necessary. But they always acted as if Panos were necessary, continuing to employ them as field laborers. They did not for a moment hesitate, so far as I could see, to invite Pano leaders to help accost the government minister. Nor were the losses and gains, on either the Warrior or Pano side, in any way livelihood-threatening; they never went much beyond the symbolic into the practical. The Pano response to their initial exclusion from the Sibhomundiro more or less removed the issue from the field of confrontational politics; they built their own Sibhomundiro. When the Panos took over the festive part of the Goma Purnomi celebrations, no Warrior was in any practical way harmed. At worst, the Warrior nose was out of joint. If jobs or land had been at stake, I believe they would have fought harder. Rewards and penalties were trivial, as they were when the Panos lost the privilege of being the village band. In neither case was anyone put out of a living or out of a job. Both sides sometimes behaved as if the pot was about to boil over, but they never let it do so.

There was another reason, still in the domain of rewards and penalties, that kept the lid firmly on the Pandora's box of political modernity. Bisipara people all were afraid of the police. That fear now seems quite straightforward, almost wholesome, when it is placed against the background of police states, secret police, people who disappear, and fanatical true believers operating in the no-man's-land between freedom-fighting, terrorism, and crime, both elsewhere and in India. In Bisipara, people knew that the police could be quite brutal when they questioned suspects; they also knew that police visits could be expensive and that a suitable gift was a better protection than innocence. But for the most part they saw the police as part of the raj, the government, about which they were quite ambivalent. On the one hand, they did not want the hand of government in village affairs if they could avoid it. But on the other hand, the raj still was adorned with the ancient notion of the protector, the bringer of order, an ultimate source of benevolence. They seemed to have a confused notion of police and government, but this confusion was, in fact, quite realistic. The raj and its police *were* both predators and protectors. In Bisipara, neither side in this contest between clean castes and Panos believed it could get exactly what it wanted out of the government; both sides had long experience of official corruption. But neither side could have contemplated with equanimity the prospect of an entirely new and different regime. In that sense people in Bisipara were not revolutionaries, nor did they think that the essential part of their world was falling apart.

The guarded legitimacy that Bisipara people still accorded to the raj had its origins partly in the commonsensical habit of calculating the costs of things and partly in a sense of awe, which came mostly from the rulers' remoteness. Although no longer non-Indians, the rulers, as they were seen in Bisipara, were another breed of people. Even in the mid-1950s no native of the Kondmals held a position of responsibility in the administration, with the exception of one man, a Christian, whose family had come to Bisipara after the turn of the century and still had a house there. That man apart, no one in Bisipara could have been considered middle class. All senior officials came from districts outside Phulbani, many of them from other parts of India. Of the five collectors who ruled in Phulbani in the years I was there, only one was an Oriya.

The significance of such remoteness is that it makes rationality in government easier. In theory, proper bureaucrats working in their offices have no kinsfolk, no friends, no co-religionists, and are blind to the metaphorical kinship of ethnicity. Being remote, they can be impersonal, and, once someone has told them what ends they must achieve, they can calculate the most effective way to deploy resources to achieve those ends. Of course, the real world is not like that, and actual bureaucrats, including outsiders, may well go in for nepotism or be corrupted in other ways. Nevertheless, in places like the Kondmals in the 1950s, if officials were corrupted it was mainly a matter of money; it was not religious or ethnic affiliation or even simple nepotism. Bisipara people knew that the sub-inspector who came to the village during the temple entry affair was a Brahmin; they did not for a moment suggest that his caste had anything to do with the way he disposed of the matter.

But their world was changing; the power of government was no longer exclusively in the hands of administrators. In the 1950s the Kondmals and Phulbani district followed more advanced areas of Orissa and began to acquire home-grown politicians. One principle of democracy is that government should not be remote from the people. A practical consequence of introducing democratic institutions into Bisipara was that politicians, if not political institutions, became more familiar. Some politicians remained distant figures. The Raja of Kalahandi, who represented the parliamentary constituency in which Bisipara lay, was still a remote and awesome person, even though the attribute that got him elected—being a king—was a well-understood form of the raj. But other people in politics were not so remote; they were familiar, even distressingly familiar. The villagers knew all too much about, for example, Gondho Sahani and the other Pano, Balunki Sahani, who stood in the Congress interest and then had a job with the Congress party, and the Distiller businessman, Basu Pradhan, who became chairman of the elected village council. None of these men inspired trust or respect, let alone awe. Their presence made the raj itself somewhat less awesome, and to a slight degree diminished the legitimizing distance that convinced ordinary people not to meddle with government. Nor could the clean castes any longer feel sure they could rely on the raj to be, mostly by default, on their side.

Indeed, in some ways the raj under which they now lived obviously was not on their side. There was the social worker that the villagers called "the Harijan inspector." They saw him as an official. The government had produced the title *Harijan* and insisted that it was politically relevant. Touring ministers and senior local officials appeared to jump higher than anyone would have expected when the Panos maneuvered them into doing so. Those few clean-caste people in Bisipara who made themselves familiar with the Congress regime and with India's new constitution had even more cause for disquiet. Since the new rulers had past injustices to undo, they biased the situation to favor less privileged categories, such as Adibasis (tribal people, like the Konds) and untouchables. Some places in schools and universities were reserved for them; so were some much sought-after government jobs, such as office peon, schoolteacher, or policeman. The electoral process was skewed by quotas; all elected bodies, from the local panchayat to the state and national legislatures, had places reserved for candidates in the disadvantaged categories. The parliamentary constituency in which Bisipara lay had two seats in the 1950s, one open (won by the former Raja of Kalahandi) and the other reserved for a scheduled tribe candidate (won by a Kond). The assembly constituency had one seat reserved for a scheduled caste person.

In several ways the situation seemed poised to lend itself to communalism and communal strife. Elections everywhere are remarkable for the degree to which, from behind a facade of reason, candidates (some of them true believers and some of them cynical) manage to appeal to mindless emotion. The conditions that make this inevitable—the technical difficulties of communicating through rational argument with a large number of diverse people all at once—were intensified in places like Orissa at that time, more especially in such districts as Phulbani. Distances were great; there were no means of mass communication in rural areas, so candidates had to go on the stump, poor ones on a bicycle and those better off in a jeep; and above all, the great mass of the electorate had no class-based ideological leanings. Name recognition helped. If a raja stood for election in an area of the state where a small kingdom had existed up to 1948, he was likely to win. Well-known freedom fighters had a similar advantage in coastal districts where the Congress movement had been effective.

Candidates who did not have those advantages looked for "vote banks," groups of people who were thought likely to vote the same way, preferably reachable through some influential person in the group. Campaigners' folk wisdom insisted that candidates must themselves belong to the majority community in the constituency, which in effect meant caste. Some constituencies in tribal areas had a distribution appropriate for that strategy. But it did not have much effect, since all parties put up candidates from the majority caste. In other places the strategy could not be effectively followed, since no one caste was more than a minority in the total population. That distribution favored the reverse selection tactic: pick a candidate who would not be identified with any caste or community (as was true of a freedom fighter or a raja).

It might still have made sense, even under these adverse demographic conditions, for politicians to make use of ethnic prejudice. Scapegoating, a tactic of politicians attempting to ride to power in Britain or France as the resolute foes of colored immigrants, was not, to my knowledge, used at that time. The Harijan issue itself might have served that purpose, since the four-fifths of the population who were not Harijans were mostly against giving them privileges. But the issue was not then salient, and the parties, even if they had wished, did not have the machinery to make it so. I suspect that the Harijans, ironically, were protected from being used in that way by their own ineffectiveness. They were not, at least in Orissa, independently organized. Down in the districts there were social workers, like Phulbani's Harijan inspector, and there was an organization at the state level. But in Orissa there was no network of agents and committees that might have been mobilized for electoral purposes and that might have made some politicians more attentive to the Harijan cause and given others the weapon of prejudicial scapegoating.

Nor were there any politically prominent untouchables with reputations that might be used one way or the other (as heroes or bogeymen), as Al Sharpton or Louis Farrakhan are sometimes

used in American politics. Even those who were elected to reserved seats mostly sat there by grace and favor of the party and
the open-seat candidate, and were by no means ideological campaigners in the Harijan interest. There were no Ambedkars
among them. Candidates with inclinations toward that kind of
militancy would probably not have been selected in the first
place.

There were other and more general influences at work to in-
hibit ideological fervor, whether over Harijans, Gandhian issues
in general, or anything at all. In the legislature the fires of ideal-
ism burned brightly in some communist members, in the few
socialists, and in a decreasing number of members of the Congress party. I do not mean that all the rest were corrupt and self-
serving, although some of them certainly were. I mean that most
of the altruism that fired them was for their own constituencies.
It is in the nature of representatives to look in that direction, if
only to secure re-election. They talked grandly, on appropriate
occasions, about major social reforms ("implementing the plan"
was the key phrase), but most of their actions were driven by
parochial pragmatism at best, sometimes by greed. In that respect they were like the people of Bisipara.

Government from Below

Most politicians at state level had nothing to gain by systematically exploiting ethnic hostilities, and any who might have
been true believers in (or against) the Harijan cause did not have
the means to do so. In local politics too, at the level of the village,
although no love was lost between the Warriors and Panos, and
although passion frequently surfaced in words and sometimes in
actions, there was no sign of the kind of moral fervor that leads
both to self-sacrifice and to genocidal tendencies.

When I went back to Bisipara in 1959 after four years away, the
winds of change had blown a little, wafting into the village an
odor of modernity that many people found somewhat disagree-

able. Here is an account (written by Debohari, and abbreviated in translation) of one such change. The text clearly conveys the mistrust which the villagers had for official altruism.

In accordance with the development plans of the Orissa government, everywhere gram panchayats are being established. Here, in 1956, the two muthas of Besringia and Betimendi were allotted one panchayat. It has nineteen members elected by the villagers, and their job is to petition the panchayat, in writing or orally, for whatever development work they consider necessary in their own villages. The panchayat is supposed to acquaint the government with these needs and, according to the government's decision, the panchayat may get on with the work. Government servants are not allowed to stand.

Several people came forward in the village as candidates. Madhia and Dino would have got most votes, but they withdrew, not wanting to contest one another. Dino would have been best because he speaks without fear to government officials; Madhia is more timid. There were a lot of meetings and finally the Bisoi [the Besringia sirdar] and some of the leading men persuaded Dino and Madhia to withdraw and urged everyone to vote for Basu Pradhan, saying, "How can you two keep going to Phulbani and fighting it out with the officials? But he lives there; he's not timid; he can face them. He's sure to be appointed *sarpanch* [chairman], and then our village has a chance of getting some work done." That was how Basu Pradhan became sarpanch.[2] He arranged to come down for a meeting in Bisipara every Monday. Gondho Sahani was appointed secretary and they say he gets a salary of Rs. 40 a month.[3]

First they set up a weekly market in Bisipara, and it ran for a couple of years (in the dry season) and then it faded away.

After that the government decided to breed fish in the pond in Hatopodera. If the government orders it, how is the panchayat to say no? Money was sanctioned, and some excavation was done to deepen the pond and it was seeded with fish. But

[2] According to a text written by another person, Basu took the initiative and gave Dino and Madhia a "sweetener" to withdraw their names. The sweetener, villagers said, was to be handed on to Sri Ramchandro's temple; but it was not.

[3] Debohari, who wrote this text, was a schoolmaster, which was a prestigious occupation. At that time his monthly salary was Rs. 30.

the water dried up in the hot weather, and they had to sell what fish they could salvage. If they had taken the trouble to seal off the ditch that drained the pond, the project might have been a success.

They also made a cattle pound, so we hear. An official came down and asked about the pound and Gondho pointed to Basu Pradhan's cattle shed. How much money they got to build a pound and what they did with it, nobody knows.

We hear they get a monthly allowance to keep the village clean. But we already pay our sweeper woman to do this, and nobody knows anything about the panchayat giving her a wage.

They meet in Basu Pradhan's house, but nobody knows what they do. They don't settle disputes. If something like that happens, the Bisoi and the leading men help settle it.

Every panchayat has a gram sevak [village level worker or VLW]. They have to tour the panchayat area and inform the government of the needs of the people—a well, a school, a dispensary, and so on. They also teach Japanese cultivation and how to manure rice plants and they bring improved seeds. But only one man in a hundred listens to what they say.[4]

The sarpanch has not done what the government promised. People do not trust him or the secretary. If there's an election, Basu Pradhan will lose. If the government would allow the sirdar to stand, he would win it. So far, we have not got much benefit from the panchayat.

The writer, Debohari, seems determinedly pessimistic, if not cynical. But this is a text, Debohari thinking back, not an objective history. Nor should this account, insofar as it may be accurate, be taken as representative of the rest of India; statutory democracy may have fared better elsewhere. These were early days (a decade after independence) and Bisipara is farther into the backwoods than most Indian villages. Nevertheless, one begins to discern—albeit more as allegory than as evidence—some features that go along with attempts to institute government from

---

[4] "Japanese cultivation" was the villagers' term. Besides the use of improved seed and fertilizer, seedlings were planted in straight lines instead of the higgledy-piggledy pattern that was customary. In that year I knew of only two fields that were cultivated in that manner. Both were large and owned by wealthy men.

below and to extend the boundary of effective citizenship. One can also understand how the dent in Bisipara's generally conservative outlook remained so small, and one can see why civil society—the communities within which people trust one another to do their duty—remained organized mostly at the molecular level, so at speak. Also very visible is the firm expectation that opportunism will be encountered everywhere.

After independence, as early as 1952, the Planning Commission (in the First Five-Year Plan) was discussing ways to involve the people in economic and social development programs. In part this policy emerged from Gandhi's ideology of the self-contained and self-governing village community (a proposal written only as a recommendation into the constitution and implemented to different degrees by different states). In part the notion came, also as an ideology, from "bootstrap" theories about community progress and popular participation advertised in India initially by the work of Albert Mayer, an American architect and town planner, in his "pilot development project" at Etawah (begun in 1948). The call for popular involvement came also from a grossly overburdened administration: overburdened because in addition to the revenue and law-and-order functions of British days, it was now also charged with effecting economic and social reform. The hope was that if people participated in deciding what would be done and therefore implicitly gave their consent, the administrators would be less encumbered with the burden of persuasion and enforcement. Community development would be achieved through local leadership and through voluntary participation, the people themselves deciding what should be done and carrying it out. The role of government, personified by community development agencies and the National Extension Service (set up in 1953), would be to facilitate and assist, not to direct.

In Debohari's text one sees these administrative intentions being put into action, and from his comments one can read off the villagers' profile of government at that time. There is evidently still a vast distance between raj and people, no hint that in independent India people have somehow become the raj. Debohari understands the intended connection between development and the panchayat; the panchayat exists to make known to the government what the villagers want—"a well, a school, a dispensary, and so on." The elected representative puts the demand to the panchayat, which in turn "acquaints" the government, which then grants or refuses the petition.

Nor is there an indication that Debohari thinks of government as a facilitator, or even as well disposed. Government is more like an adversary than an ally. The villagers look for a chairman who can "fight it out" with government, a person who is not timid, who can speak "without fear" to officials.

Notice also that making a petition is not seen as planning from below or *government* from below—phrases that would mean as little to them as they do anywhere outside populist rhetoric. "If the government orders it, how is the panchayat to say no?" There is no indication that the panchayat's duty is to filter and consolidate or set the demands that come before it in an order of priority. It merely "acquaints" the government and leaves the decisions to it. The most one can expect is the chairman's informal influence with officials. The raj is not a function to be shared down a hierarchy. It is there as an entity, solid, substantial and personlike (even if one does not know exactly who makes the decisions).

All the Bisipara projects mentioned (except perhaps the market) were ordered by the government. The initiative came from above (thus giving the villagers the luxury of blaming others when projects failed). In this, Bisipara's experience was far from unique. Planning all too often is a hasty business, everyone working against deadlines, both administrative and fiscal. To wait for ideas to come up from below is to court failure. Moreover, since grass-roots schemes are likely to be diverse, it is difficult to consolidate them and reduce them to manageable numbers and so stay within a budget. Proposals have to be submitted to higher authorities, and it is only sensible for lower officials not to give their superiors a headache by sending up a disorderly or extravagant shopping list. Thus intermediate levels in the hierarchy like to decide what those down below would demand, if they were articulate enough (or what they can be manipulated into demanding). Then deadlines are met and reputations for administrative efficiency are preserved and projects are financed. The only problem is that the "customer" gets what is convenient for the store's management.

Debohari's text also makes clear that Bisipara's entrepreneurial spirit is anything but a conscious anti-socialist, pro-free-enterprise ideology. The idea of impersonal market forces, the hidden hand that must be allowed to eliminate arbitrary decisions by authorities, is entirely absent. The villagers, knowing very well that there is not enough for everyone, have no conception of a market that stabilizes the process of distribution. One does not petition market forces. They do not see themselves as buyers and sellers in a marketplace but as petitioners before a king, an adjudicator, a *person* with authority who will make the decision. One either competes with other petitioners to win the authority's attention or tries to outsmart the authority itself. It might indeed be argued that this is exactly how interest-group politics work everywhere and that the neoclassical "laws" of the market are as insubstantial in politics as they are in economic activity, because the "laws" are always being bent to someone's advantage.

"Someone's advantage" is the key phrase. Notice in the text how the gap (in communication and in trust) between peasants and officials has reappeared between peasants and their elected representatives, in this case the chairman, Basu Pradhan, and his appointed secretary, Gondho Sahani. Both these men were born in the village, and Gondho still lived there. Basu maintained a house in Bisipara but spent his time at the district headquarters, where he had another house and a shop. Gondho was a Pano. Caste affiliation did not help Basu; he was a Distiller. Both men followed a lifestyle that marked them as outsiders in part. Gondho had been a policeman and in the 1950s was an active politician. Basu was a businessman, prospering on contracts which he obtained from government, mainly development projects like road and bridge improvements or school buildings. Because they believed he had influence with officials, gained through his business activities, the villagers accepted Basu as chairman of the panchayat. But these same activities made him suspect, and his performance as sarpanch, Debohari asserts, merely confirmed the suspicion that he would serve his own interests at their expense. He had, in other words, sold out, and he was using villagers as instruments to forward his own career in politics or in business, or more likely in a combination that made politics a source of profit.

Self-serving opportunism at public expense was condemned in Bisipara, as it is everywhere else. But it was expected. Debohari implies that the villagers would have been happy to have their sirdar as chairman of the council if the regulations had made it possible. But the implied comparison with the unsuitable Basu is itself an opportunist argument, for I have several texts, by Debohari and others, which accuse the sirdar of using his own office to enrich himself. Even the raising of money to fight the case against the Panos in court fell under that kind of suspicion. I am sure also that the Panos frequently asked themselves what personal benefits their leaders were getting out of the affair. Moral fervor is not easily aroused when everyone is constantly asking who has a piece of the action.

Opportunism was built into Bisipara's cultural foundations. Everyone cheats when they get the chance. A more detailed version of the Pano myth quoted earlier speaks of them being urged by the Warriors to trick the Konds who lived in Bisipara (then called Talopara):

> The courage of the four sons and grandsons of Mondano and Gopalo Sahani was renowned. A message was sent to fetch them. "You can mingle with the Konds and you are their advisers. Therefore come. In Talopara Biniki and Saniki Kohoro are murdering Oriyas. Feed them liquor and win their faith and murder them. Then we can settle there together." So the four men settled in Gonjagura, and with liquor they tamed the Konds. When Biniki and Saniki were drunk, they killed them with battle axes, and brought their heads to the Boralo deity at Bolscoopa.

Perhaps the implied opportunism (and the tactical use of alcohol) is why, thirty or forty years after the event, people still talked of how the wily Ollenbach tricked and captured the Pano outlaws.

Penny-wise Politics

I set out to explain a non-event: Why did the small initial foray into violence between ethnic groups in Bisipara not escalate? The main answer, which has appeared in a variety of contexts, was that all those concerned—Warriors, Panos, their leaders, the officials, the politicians at state and local levels—were accustomed to counting the cost. This habit of mind, I suggest, inhibits moral fervor. A resolute pragmatism, together with pervasive suspicions that opportunism is everywhere, make it hard to be a true believer, for whatever cause.

In what circumstances, then, is that kind of outlook on the world likely to be maintained? It might be said that this concern for *personal* utility (and an implied unconcern with the well-being of others) is a function of both the Hindu idea of *personal* salvation and of the caste system's toleration of difference. That seems unlikely. Collective mindless brutality, both within Hinduism and towards other religions, is too much in evidence. Nor could one explain why upholders of Hinduism became self-sacrificing freedom fighters.

I think that pragmatism and opportunism prevailed in Bisipara because for a long time that design for living had worked sufficiently well for a sufficient number of people. It worked because both the Panos and all the other castes in Bisipara came to the Kondmals as entrepreneurs, parasites on a society that had different values, and they continued to a significant extent to be so, despite having an "official" existence in caste-framed communities as landowners and laborers and specialists of various kinds (priests, herdsmen, barbers, washermen, and the rest). The entrepreneurial spirit—pragmatic opportunism—was enhanced by the coming of the British administration. The British pacified the area and opened up trade. The new administration proved a happy hunting ground for indigenous political and economic entrepreneurs. Not least, also, it set a tone that fostered pragmatism and, beyond setting a tone, used its police to damp down fervor.

There were two other reasons why this design for living survived in good health down into the 1950s. First, those who followed it had to work hard and had little time or energy for reflective dissatisfaction. Some did well and others did less well, but the system did not produce a desperate proletariat (the Boida outlaws being possibly a very small step in that direction). Nor, second, did it produce that hothouse for abrupt revolution, an educated, insufficiently employed middle class. Bisipara's own semi-professional politicians were anything but ideologues; they were, certainly in the opinion of their fellow villagers, on the make like everyone else.

But Bisipara did have a revolution in which the Warriors were dispossessed and privilege was dispersed. In other places, including some in India, dispossessed gentry became true believers in themselves and in their class and resorted to violence. But Bisipara's landowners were not gentry; their lifestyle was too humble to deserve that word. Nevertheless, one might have expected that the spectacle of Panos apparently elevated by government favor would have produced a backlash of the kind that from time to time erupts in violence elsewhere in India over the special privileges in education and government jobs granted to Harijans and tribals. That grievance indeed was very much in Bisipara's public domain; the Warriors and their allies talked about it frequently and heatedly.

But mostly they *talked*. They did not take resolute collective action. As I said, they often seemed more like actors in a play than people for whom real power was at stake. They fought over symbols. They were cardplayers who never cashed in their chips, not because they wanted to prolong that particular game but because everyone knew that to convert the game into reality would hurt them all. I think the truth is that, for all the sound and fury from Debohari and other Warriors, the ingrained pragmatic outlook had extended itself into the post-1947 world of opportunities, and everyone, whatever the caste, Harijan movement and Harijan privileges notwithstanding, was doing more or less equally well (or badly) under the new regime. Everyone was busy learning how to milk the new institutions, and the opportunity to do so in reality was not, despite the Harijan rhetoric, mainly distributed according to caste.

Bisipara, always encased in pragmatism, had been opened up to a wider world that still was pragmatic with respect both to economics and to politics. The old ideology of social form, the dharma, the set of ideas that supported Warrior dominance, was much eroded. Moreover, given that Bisipara was an entrepôt, that ideology, although formally dominant, had by no means eliminated the habitual prejudice in favor of calculated utility. The effective political world had mostly gone outside the village, but the open society's ideologies—whether Gandhian or socialist or Harijan or any other true belief—had in the 1950s not much penetrated into Bisipara. Besides, the wider world, at least that part which intruded into Bisipara, was itself becoming permeated with pragmatism. Meanwhile, Bisipara people, Harijans and the rest, were getting on with the necessary business of coping with everyday survival. That was why they chose a noninstrumental way to express collective hostilities, doing so mainly through cultural performances that left lives and livelihoods undamaged.

8

The Civility of Indifference

Bisipara's story, apart from one small twist, which I will keep until the end, has now been told. This chapter is a coda, an addition to the book's essential part. It will review what the people of Bisipara did and how (I think) their minds worked. It will also describe what was in my mind as I constructed their story. This, then, is an *apologia pro historia sua*; or it is an anticipatory strike against critics, or a narcissistic metanarrative, or perhaps just a methodological appendix.

When we try to make sense of human beings and what they do, we have an apparent advantage over those who want to understand the tides, metal fatigue, or tomato blight. This advantage is introspection. Metals and tomatoes and tides do not have minds, but people do; and we believe we can look into their minds. People make meanings; we can share those meanings. This is the method of empathy, the instant and *intuitive* placing of oneself in the mind of the other person. (Of course, it is a flight of fancy; the act is *intro*spection—looking *inward*. One can see into no one's mind except one's own, and even that is sometimes doubtful.)

In the presently fashionable posture of self-debasement before the Other, the notion that one can enter another person's mind by deducing meaning and sentiment from behavior has become morally suspect. When I write about Bisipara and its people, it is said, I am in fact unwittingly writing about myself, because I, the naive author, am the one who stands revealed by my text, not the Other, despite the fact that my text is ostensibly a description of the Other's beliefs and values. Even worse, I am exhibiting arrogance, imperialism; I am being patronizing, and I am covertly asserting a right to dominate. According to this conceit, I, as an anthropologist, write a sinister mixture of fiction and self-advocacy, producing an imaginary construct that is shaped by the axes (political, economic, ethnic, gendered, or whatever else) that, consciously or unconsciously, I am always grinding.

Of course I am revealed in what I write. Of course I grind axes. It happens always and everywhere, and the breast-beaters themselves are not exempt. To varying degrees self-revelation and self-interest pervade all social science writing. This idea is hardly new; it lies at the center of the sociology of knowledge. Ideas are not insulated from social context. It is well known that we do not simply report "the facts." We would not be doing so even if, machinelike, we reproduced nothing but the statements of our informants, claiming to draw no conclusions. Our reporting would still be selective and would indicate where we expected truth to be found. To assert that the anthropologist's role is limited to a minimalist form of description—mere reportage of what people say, raw material without analysis—is simple-minded if not disingenuous. The choice of material is itself a form of analysis, and those who claim to respect the Other by merely reporting and refusing to analyze what the Other says are, at best, deceiving themselves.

Every writer is in part a prisoner of his or her time and culture, but not entirely so, not all writers, not always, not equally. One and the same time, one and the same society, manage to produce alternative versions of the truth, and for some of these truths there is an objective world against which the different versions can be tested. At least some statements are empirically falsifiable, without reference to the bias of their authors. My writing of Bisipara, like the life I lived there, is and was colored by my end-of-empire background, my class origins, and by the many other things that have shaped my attitudes and my thinking. But that is not all that can be said. The *argumentum ad hominem* does not eliminate the question of objective accuracy; it is a simple evasion of the issue. In short, the propositions in this memoir are not *only* rhetoric; they also are offered within a framework that, at least in principle, invites empirical testing. It is or it is not the case that the people of Bisipara in the 1950s habitually exercised moderation in their behavior. It is or is not the case that this restraint was the product of their experiences as wheelers and dealers, their perception of the raj, the state of mind characteristic of a caste system, and so forth. These propositions are true or false quite independently of the biases and motives of the person making them. Only when the propositions are empirically demonstrated to be in error does it become appropriate to ask what bias might have contributed to the error.

Empathy is experienced as unmediated and effortless access to the truth, apparently achieved without step-by-step deductive reasoning, a kind of clairvoyance. The experience, however, is deceptive, because under the seemingly instantaneous intuition lies a deductive model that links an event (for example, a mishap) or words (an expletive) with the actor's or the speaker's state of mind (irritation). But the model's working is so slick that the model itself remains mostly inexplicit and therefore unexamined. There is nothing provisional about an intuition; no systematic rechecking of the logic; just the sensation of instant truth. An ethnography written in the mode of empathy, if well written, seems to carry its own conviction, as a novel does. It is rich in texture, portraying people in the round; it "rings true," so that to ask for corroborating evidence would seem crass. The ethnography has then become a work of art and its message is privileged, being exempted from empirical testing and the demand for evidence. This text is not in that category: no clairvoyance, not a work of art.

It is appropriate to test an intuition (and an ethnography).[1] Subsequent events and actions may later falsify what introspec-

---

[1] David Jacobson (1991) did ask for evidence, and the result is an entertaining parade of some anthropological emperors (and one empress) inadequately clothed.

tion had said was in even one's own mind. The risk of error increases when the image is projected into the mind of another person, and for obvious reasons it becomes greater still when that person's mind has been shaped by another culture and a set of experiences foreign to the would-be intuitor. Intuition—*Verstehen*—is good for getting ideas, inventing hypotheses. It will not serve to validate them. Empathy does not explain; it only asserts.

Explanation requires a step-by-step procedure, which has four components: a problem to be explained (why did Bisipara people behave with moderation in the Harijan conflict?), a covering law or general proposition (certain prior conditions induce moderation), a demonstration that these conditions applied (in Bisipara), and a deduction that, if the covering law is correct, there should be other manifestations (of moderation) besides the one in question. The general proposition employed in the present analysis incorporates a variant of the economists' expected-utility framework. That framework uses a few simple intuited assumptions about human nature and from them explains (or predicts) conduct. The assumptions are, in the words of one of the model's stricter constructionists, Lionel Robbins, "so much the stuff of our everyday experience that they have only to be stated to be recognized as obvious" (1937, 79). Some of these assumptions are indeed familiar in everyday culture (they are slightly less familiar when translated into technical language): people want things (things have *utility*); people want some things more than others (they have an order of *preference*); different things in different combinations are equally acceptable (discovered by *indifference analysis*); people use their heads to work out the most effective way to get what they want with the resources at their disposal (they are *rational economizers*); and, beyond a certain point, the more they have of something the less incentive they have to get still more of it (*marginal utility*); things are in short supply, so there is *competition* for them; and this competition is made orderly through *markets*, where suppliers and their customers bargain, establish prices, and so create order by adjusting supply and demand.

In this kind of discourse the actors are not textured; they remain thin and hypothetical, rational marionettes that move only within the limits of the framework. The intuited motivation from which the expected-utility model starts is a plain, unelaborated, and unqualified assertion, which is best described as crass. For example, it may be taken as a self-evident truth that all rational people strive for money (or honor or power or a place in heaven or anything else scarce enough to be valued as a prize). The motivation being given, and all other motivations excluded, variations in context can then be used to explain variations in behavior. Given a standard incentive, rational people—people who think about how best to deploy the means at their disposal to attain a given end—would have no choice about how to behave in a particular context, because only one choice would be rational. In that way context can be made to predict or explain or even engineer behavior. Car pooling, for instance, might be a function of the parking fee; the higher the fee, the greater the incentive to put up with the inconvenience of sharing rides.

The intuited motivation (maximizing utility) is always taken to be the exclusive motivation; economic man is not modeled as having a tinge of conscience. But there is no larger assumption that the intuited motivation is necessarily always the case everywhere (although much that is written seems to take it for granted that rational choice of the materially self-advantaging kind is the invariant reality). Statements are always provisional, hypothetical propositions that subsequently will be upheld or dismissed by evidence. The limits of the model's usefulness—that is, its explanatory scope—must be established empirically by showing where it does, or does not, explain past conduct or predict future conduct. Whenever the selected motivation—the assumed "utility"—is not in fact what moves people, then the model will neither predict nor explain conduct. The model that works well enough for car pooling may not work so well for conduct within the family, despite the heroic simplifications of Gary Becker (1976).

Deriving motivations from the "stuff of our everyday experience" turns out to be a more complicated matter than Robbins assumed, because in everyday life utility-maximization is embedded in a matrix that contains other kinds of value. In other words, interests sometimes come into conflict with duty and do not always win. Obviously also, when people are *not* rational at all and act without calculating the consequences of what they do, the model is not applicable. Nor will it be of much use when people do not have enough information to make the required computations. These weaknesses are well known, but they are not a reason for dispensing altogether with the concept of expected utility. No model will explain everything; the task is to discover what it will explain.

I should make it clear that I am not talking about human nature in general, nor directly about the motivational patterns of individuals, but about what the people of Bisipara, at the time I knew them, believed to be the way minds "naturally" worked. In doing so I follow Robbins, making deductions from my "everyday experience" of them. I think they too, if they had reflected on the matter, would have "recognized as obvious" the motivational configuration that I am about to describe.

The temple entry story allegorizes a *commonsense* version of the expected-utility framework, and it is this version, I believe, that prevailed in Bisipara's culture at that time. I will explain what I want *commonsense* to mean, for in a Manichean intellectual world opposing the rational economizer to the duty-bound moral person, any framework that uses the notion of commonsense (and makes room for *both* morality—of a sort—*and* for interests, blending the two and blunting the sharp edge of their difference) will easily be misunderstood.

Strictly construed, the expected-utility framework assumes that people act rationally; that is, they allocate scarce resources so as to achieve some desired end. The theory does not specify any particular kind of end, so that, for example, self-inflicted suffering intended to ensure a place in heaven would be, within the strict construal, a perfectly rational choice. (For those who do not believe there is a heaven, the choice would be a mistake, and the decision would have "procedural" but not "instrumental" ra-

tionality.) In the same way, those who exterminate Jews or Gypsies or any other racially marked population solely in order to
"keep the race pure" would be, given that goal, acting rationally.
Even if their biology was all astray (because the "race" was
already a total genetic hodgepodge) and they therefore lacked
instrumental rationality, they could still have procedural rationality. In fact, of course, they usually do not. Genocidal enthusi-
asts do not stop to think. They are fanatics, mindless true believers. One could imagine a simulacrum of procedural
rationality (exterminating unclean races keeps the master race
pure), but in fact the consequences are irrelevant because the act
is defined as *intrinsically* good and therefore requires no justification.

In practice, users of the expected-utility framework generally
do limit the range of utilities they are willing to contemplate. The
most restricted procedure (and the one most commonly in use,
because it is readily quantifiable) specifies material rewards, usually profit. A slightly wider version uses power—or at least control over one's own life—as an index for utility, and this is not so
easy to quantify. A still more general version, which defies quan-
tification, is the amiable version used in Bisipara: insofar as people calculate the consequences of their actions, their first goal
usually is to avoid putting themselves or their dear ones at a
disadvantage, whether with respect to material comfort or to
dignity and reputation. The intention is to avoid a fall, not to run
the fastest. That is the commonsense framework.

More is involved. Bisipara's commonsense version of expected
utility also incorporates what at first sight appears to be an ethi-
cal rule—moderation in all things—but in fact is a rule based
more on expediency than on morality. In this philosophy avoiding excess has nothing to do with virtue; it simply is seen as the
smart thing to do. The rule regulates conflict. *Expected utility*
(which is, of course, a God term) unfolds a world that is in essence adversarial, a competitor's world. The default mode is conflict. One should expect, until experience shows otherwise, any
encounter to be a contest for limited resources, out of which will

emerge a winner and a loser. But the expected-utility conduct that I observed in Bisipara (and surely it exists elsewhere) was adversarial in a very controlled manner. It was by no means a war of all against all, not petty capitalism red in tooth and claw. In fact, it was not so much a war as it was a well-ordered contest conducted within a framework of rules. I do not mean only that there were courts of law, inspectors of weights and measures, regulations governing what was rightly an object of trade and what was not, and various other codified restraints on raw opportunism. A no less significant regulatory determinant was an attitude of mind that can be represented, somewhat inadequately, by that phrase from Tacitus, *sine ira et studio*, without anger and without zeal.

Those words do not quite catch the mentality that I want to convey. For sure, Bisipara people avoided most forms of extravagant behavior. They were not at all given to extremes of bodily indulgence, being anything but Dionysian. Konds had their bacchanalia from time to time, but not the staid Oriyas. There were some exceptions. Pano and Potter men, particularly the Panos, were drinkers. Two or three people, old men, were addicted to ganja. But for the most part people stopped short of excess. No one was an habitual gormandizer; the culinary arts were rudimentary and in any case food was rarely abundant. Nor did they have the peasant's purported admiration for hard physical work; they did not think, as we do, that the devil finds mischief for idle hands. Most of the year hands were, out of necessity, far from idle; and when they were, the weather was too hot to do anything but be idle. They worked hard when they had to, but they were not workaholics; they did not work for work's sake.

But they did have some enthusiasms. Most of them were zealous in their search for profit. They also were avid double-dealers. An outsider was always marked as a prospective pigeon, a candidate for plucking. They worked hard at cheating even one another, and everyone knew it. In that respect they were eager rule breakers. But one rule they did not often break: they habitually acted with calculated moderation, even when they put on the appearance of being impassioned. In their dealings they seldom gave in to anger, still less to sustained mindless hatred. *As is supposed to happen in the economists' world, they bestowed on their transactional opponents the status of things to be manipulated.* They did not dignify them either as persons having a moral status and deserving instant trust or, inversely (and crucially for my argument), as persons deserving hatred. The object was to emerge from an encounter with a net profit, not primarily to get the better of opponents or to humiliate them, certainly not to exterminate them. Dealing with superiors, manipulative humility (tongue-in-cheek humility) came easily to them; only fools had stiff necks.

This attitude arose from the same general and fundamental guide for proper conduct that cannot be called moral, since it involves treating persons as things. The rule was (to borrow again from the classical world) *nothing to excess.* As I said at the outset, I do not think the people I knew in Bisipara were overly endowed with altruism, nor were they rampantly egoistic, ruthlessly and unremittingly in search of individual advantage. They were tolerant of one another, not because they had highly developed and explicit notions of the individual's proper space and proper freedoms, not for positive reasons, but as a matter of habit, by default. To have been intolerant, had they thought about it, would have been judged expensive, too much trouble, a bad investment, and in the end self-destructive. Their moral horizons (the limits they set on loving and hating) were narrow and they behaved as if they had only a small stock of moral energy, which they preferred to husband for a few people and for special occasions. They distrusted heroics; they were alienated by discourse on causes and by leaders demanding sacrifice. Self-sacrifice for the greater glory of the motherland, or of god, or for the purity of the race, or, as I said, even for Gandhi's Swaraj, they would have seen as strictly for the birds, not for them. They were on a level with the pettiest of the petty bourgeoisie, quite bereft of revolutionary tendencies. Of course, this benign indifference could only be sustained to the extent that most people in their social environment possessed the same attitude; the extremes of passionate intensity would otherwise soon have corrupted that centralizing moderation. Bisipara was a very *Candide* world of cultivating one's own garden and mostly letting other people get on with cultivating theirs. This ethic of at least appearing to mind one's own business—not a feature of the zealot—survived, predictably, in the midst of contest-by-bargaining and, paradoxically, unaffected by the intimate knowledge that gossip gave them of each other's doings.

They drew narrow boundaries around their moral communities. These extended outwards in concentric circles from immediate family to other kinfolk in the caste, to neighbors, and, at the margin, to a vague category of *people like us* (often construed negatively as *not officials*). At each outer boundary the other person was to be treated more as an instrument and less as a person qualified to command moral status (that is, to benefit from the injunction "Do as you would be done by"). But, as the story shows, this tendency to increasing incivility was balanced out by the unintended civility of indifference. It was not altruism but the rationality of expected utility (a rationality internalized rather than voiced) that required them to abstain from the excesses of antagonism. The outcome was an inadvertent humanism. In that situation hatred, which is the malady of true believers and of many religions, could never have become an end in itself because it would have been seen as stupidly wasteful. Indifference took its place. "Nothing," Edmund Burke wrote, "is so fatal to religion as indifference."

Those who do not live by this commonsense version of expected utility are unwilling to think, critically and sustainedly, about the costs of what they do. Having once decided that a course of action is morally imperative, or noble, or virtuous, they do not go on to calculate the damage it might cause. In the true Gandhian style, one way is identified as "truth" and is thus defined both as unique (there is only one truth) and as self-justifying, and this way therefore cannot be costed. Intrinsic rightness precludes accounting. The story of Bisipara's racism shows this

procedure put into reverse; the deeply ingrained habit of calculating costs and benefits, putting instant morality to one side,
saved the people of Bisipara from the nastiness of ethno-racist-
religious true belief.

In certain canting, pseudo-true-believing discourses about
what is proper in the analysis of cultural and social systems, the
notions I have used of *structure*, *rationality*, *order*, and *explanation*
are condemned as illusions or hegemonic fictions. The social
world does not have a structure that gives it order, the argument
goes, and those who claim it does only do so because the claim
gives them power or aligns them with those who have power.
There is no single design for living. Plurality reigns. (Of course it
does; it always has. Outside the world of the true believer, it is
well known that no one model, whether directive or explanatory,
could anywhere suffice.)

Today the modish conception of reality is contestation; we live
in disorder and in strife, it is asserted, and the scholar who is
honest and uncorrupted not only recognizes the resulting formlessness by carefully avoiding such terms as *structure* or *function*
or even *culture* but also sees virtue nowhere but in resistance to
whoever or whatever dominates. This is eristic arrogance, a
sophist's world of argument without end, of argument for victory not for truth. Ideas in that world are *con*tested but never
tested by matching them against a reality. (If it required testing,
this episteme would be commendably heuristic. Notice an affin-
ity with science; both require sustained questioning of dogma, a
firm belief that paradoxically insists that no beliefs are firm and
every construction awaits deconstruction and reconstruction.[2])

But the people of Bisipara did not see a world of unremitting
contestation and formlessness. They, including those at the bottom of the heap, believed in cooperation, rationality, and order,
even when they did not have precisely those words in their lexi-

[2] This is, of course, an intellectual stance, not necessarily the practice. Or-
thodoxies, whether scientific or moralistic, are not easily questioned. See
Kuhn 1970.

con. They construed their world as comprising not only subaltern people but subaltern ideas as well. Neither people nor
ideas are equal; there are boss-people and there are boss-ideas.
Certainly in Bisipara they contested different versions of dharma,
the natural order of society and of the world—that was the point
of the temple entry dispute—but at the same time there was an
underlying, shared, mostly tacit, and uncontested conception of
reality, a notion of how things really did (and should) work. This
conception was not an agreed version of the dharma of orthodox
Hinduism; it was what I have here called commonsense expected
utility. It went unquestioned (but not as a true belief, because
true beliefs exist only when articulated). As I said, this conception of reality (which is something very much richer than the
plain philosophy of the fast buck) was never upheld by ser-
monizing. Occasionally its calculative features came to the surface, as in Debohari's very materialist and somewhat cynical
evaluation of the gram panchayat. More often it remained un-
voiced; it was simply taken for granted.

There is nothing puzzling, nothing abnormal, about this state
of affairs. People in Bisipara anchored their perceptions and their
actions in a definition of how the world worked, which they did
not, at that time, question. They had not yet had experiences that
would point up its disadvantages and so make them think critically about it. Above that bedrock they had layers of "less real"
realities. It is therefore to be expected that when Bisipara people
appeared to contest different versions of reality and consequently of duty (dharma enfolds both these concepts), the contestation had about it a distinct element of playacting, of not being, so to speak, in deadly earnest. The *Pano* versus *Harijan*
controversy, the example around which this memoir is built, was
conducted in Bisipara with gamelike restraint. I do not mean
they were doing it for fun; I mean that they did not see this as *the*
most important issue that faced them.

In short, underneath the overt plurality of conceptions and the
overt ideological contestation there was a single, unifying definition of reality that had to do with calculation and rationality (the

commonsense expected-utility model). This was the foundat
Bisipara's definition of how the world really worked—agr~~~
on, acted upon, and therefore authentic. Above it were other versions, which were contested and ranked as more important and
less important. If anything should be called illusory in this situation, it is not the value set on moderation and order; it is the
mimed contestation.

The people of Bisipara also seemed to work with a straightfor-
wardly empiricist conception of cause and effect: beliefs and
values are connected to actions, actions have consequences, and
these consequences feed back onto the beliefs and values.
Knowledge is the fruit of experience. People behaved as if they
thought that any state of affairs can be explained by, among
other things, the antecedent actions that have been taken. One
copes with the world by seeking cause-and-effect connections.
The beliefs and values that one has are designs for living. From
time to time they are put to the test of application, and one can
expect that sooner or later those that are perceived to hurt more
than they help will be discarded. (Recall the young men of clean
caste; they did not go of their own accord into the street of the
Panos, but, sensitive to the wind of change, they would accompany me there. Their elders would not.)

From a postmodernist point of view, Bisipara people were re-
actionaries; they were naive positivists, making sense of their experiences by modeling them as cause and consequence, seeking
explanations, and inadvertently allowing themselves to be
guided by a defunct episteme. Vibrant postmodernism—its upholders seem to enjoy the frisson of righteous audacity—brands
explanation as a form of disrespect for the Other, because explanation makes the Other a product and reduces the Other's
agency. There is an answer. No one has unlimited powers of
agency, and everyone sometime is disempowered by circumstances or by other people. Why should we pretend this is not
so?

In the course of reporting the conduct of the people of Bisipara
and its antecedent thinking, I have followed their episteme, look-

ing for explanations. Undeniably the first task is to describe the understanding they had of their sociocultural world. But interpretation of behavior (that is, a description of the actor's understandings without an attempt to explain) is only half the task; we should be able to say not only what people think but also why they think it. Their understanding is itself the product of past experiences, and the two-way connection between beliefs and experience can be caught in empirically testable propositions. In that manner I have endeavored to explain why moderation played such a central role in Bisipara's philosophy.

My project has been narrow, staying close to one set of particulars. I have looked at one place at one time, at Bisipara as it was forty years ago, a time when the people there seemed poised to take off into communal violence. I have explained why that did not happen, why they did not lose their heads and did not try to kill one another. The argument I have made about them was that certain taken-for-granted ways of coping with everyday life, the habit of calculating material payoffs and, above all, being wary of excess, tended to limit the space available for the extremes of ethnic hatred. This deeply internalized feature of Bisipara's lifestyle, a similar pragmatism among officials and, most significantly, among politicians (who might otherwise have been a source for righteous extremism), a coercive order-producing centralism (the raj, mainly the police), and, not least, an everyday familiarity with the domesticated, unexplosive racial attitudes of a localized and still largely unpoliticized caste system—all of these attributes, taken together with the capacity of existing institutions to more or less meet everyday expectations, account for Bisipara's people benignantly letting slip an opportunity to behave like true believers.

The tale has been about the evils that are latent in true-believership and an uncompromising moral rectitude, and about why these evils were not, in one particular instance, manifested. This is not, of course, to claim that the inverse of true-believership and moral rectitude, which would be a thoroughgoing opportunism unsoftened by altruism, could provide a style of life that is desirable or even possible. What they did right in Bisipara at that time was avoid the extremes.

What, finally, have I said about the people of Bisipara? My purpose in this book has been more to depict them and their outlook on life than to theorize about ethnicity or methods of analysis. From one point of view, that of activist politicians and of words-on-paper activist intellectuals (leftists or rightists), they appear to be political innocents, brimful with false conscious-ness, a barefoot bourgeoisie, simple-minded, mere children who had not yet experienced the painful ecstasies that reward true belief, the ruthless dedication of the self, and the unflinching sac-rifice of innocent others to the cause of the coming revolution— or of the nation, the race, or the one true faith. From another direction, however, they emerge as people matured beyond the stage of mindless enthusiasms, grown up, sophisticated, rational, wary, nobody's fools (but at the same time stopping somewhat short of cynicism), confident (within narrow circles) of each other's kindness and sincerity, and, beyond that, compassionate in a limited way, even public-spirited to the extent they saw ben-efits in being so—unexamined lives, perhaps, but surely worth living.

All I have done in this book is make sense of what I saw hap-pen in Bisipara in the 1950s. I do not know if life there, forty years later, still rests on that rock of quiet pragmatism. Possibly the rock has shifted, for I read in the *Statesman Weekly* (June 18, 1994) a brief report of recent disorders in Phulbani district. A Harijan had been murdered when he entered a Shiva temple, and further killings, fourteen in all, had taken place. The killers were reported to be "Kandhas," who "are said to be a fierce group," but the two villages mentioned are in fact populated by Oriyas, as Bisipara is. (It is possible, but unlikely, that during the last forty years all the Oriyas went away and Konds came in. More likely, the journalist did not know that the Kondmals con-tained Oriya villages.) The article goes on to link the disorders (not, however, explaining what the connection was) to a demand that the name of the district be changed from Baud-Phulbani to Kandhmala and that the status of the constituency be changed from "Scheduled Caste (reserved)" to "Scheduled Tribe (reserved)." Both these demands suggest that local politicians have discovered that ethnic righteousness, when it leads to violence, can be exploited and made to yield a political payoff.

References

AVARD
    1962   *Panchayat Raj as the Basis of Indian Polity.* New Delhi: AVARD.
Becker, Gary S.
    1976   *The Economic Approach to Human Behavior.* Chicago: Chicago
        University Press.
Bondurant, Joan V.
    1965 [1958]   *The Conquest of Violence.* Berkeley: University of Cali-
        fornia Press.
Burke, Kenneth
    1969   *A Grammar of Motives.* Berkeley: University of California
        Press.
Campbell, John
    1861   *Narrative of operations in the Hill Tracts of Orissa for the sup-
        pression of Human Sacrifice and Infanticide.* London: Hurst and
        Blackett.
    1864   *A Personal Narrative of Thirteen Years Service among the Wild
        Tribes of Khondistan.* London: Hurst and Blackett.
Dumont, Louis
    1970 [1966]   *Homo Hierarchicus.* London: Weidenfeld and Nicolson.
Evans-Pritchard, E. E.
    1940   *The Nuer.* Oxford: Clarendon Press.
Furnivall, J. S.
    1948   *Colonial Policy and Practice.* Cambridge: Cambridge Univer-
        sity Press.
Gilliland, Mary K.
    1986   *The Maintenance of Family Values in a Yugoslav Town.* Ann
        Arbor, Mich.: University Microfilms International.

Jacobson, David
  1991   *Reading Ethnography*. Albany: State University of New York
    Press.
The Khond Agency and the Calcutta Review.
  1849   Madras: Pharaoh.
Kuhn, Thomas
  1970   *The Structure of Scientific Revolutions*. Chicago: Chicago University Press.
Lenin, V. I.
  1975 [1920]   *"Left-Wing" Communism, an Infantile Disorder*. Peking:
    Foreign Language Press.
Macpherson, William, ed.
  1865   *Memorials of Service in India*. London: John Murray.
Misra, B. R.
  1956   *V for Vinoba*. Calcutta: Orient Longmans.
Olsen, Mary Kay Gilliland
  1993   "Bridge on the Sava: Ethnicity in Eastern Croatia, 1981–
    1991." *Anthropology of Eastern Europe Review* 11: 54–62.
Robbins, Lionel
  1932   *An Essay on the Nature and Significance of Economic Science*.
    London: Macmillan.
*Selections from the Records of the Government of India. Vol. 5. History of
the rise and progress of the operations for the suppression of Human
Sacrifice and Female Infanticide in the Hill Tracts of Orissa*
  1854   Calcutta: Bengal Military Orphan Press.
Simmel, Georg
  1964 [1955]   *Conflict and the Web of Group Affiliations*. Trans. Kurt
    H. Wolf. New York: Free Press.
Woodruff, Philip
  1963 [1953–54]   *The Men Who Ruled India*. 2 vols. London: Jonathan Cape.

Index

The names of castes are in capital letters.